THROUGH THE VALLEY OF THE SHADOW

An Anthology of Select Funeral Sermons

PRINTED IN U.S.A.

TABLE OF CONTENTS

PUBLISHER'S PREFACE

In this anthology, you will discover thirty sermons for funerals as well as four special articles and funeral service suggestions, each selected from materials contributed by members of the C.S.S. family of authors, to help the pastor in the difficult, challenging, and crucial ministry of proclaiming the gospel to those who are recently bereaved.

The sermons have been organized into five sections:

- Funeral Sermons for Suicide Victims
- Funeral Sermons for Persons Stricken Suddenly
- Funeral Sermons for the Young and Very Young
- Funeral Sermons for Other Circumstances
- Funeral Sermons for Unique Occasions

A word might be said about the final section of sermons. We finally selected the word, "unique," after scouring the *Thesaurus*, because other words seemed too dramatic to cover the range of the sermons included. In this section, you will read a sermon preached at an annual Communion memorial service for the deceased of a special group within a congregation; a sermon preached at a funeral where the pastor did not know the deceased; a sermon preached on the Sunday following the sudden death of a parishioner during the previous Sunday's worship service; and two sermons preached to a "normal Sunday morning congregation" on the topic of death and funerals.

The final section of this book provides you with articles and funeral service suggestions.

Funeral Sermons for Suicide Victims

A TRUE, MODERN PARABLE
Charles L. Koester

Preached at the funeral of a forty-four year old man who committed suicide. The writer was the victim's best personal friend as well as pastor.

†††

Opening pulpit prayer:
Father, we pray for strength for this difficult time. For these difficult moments. Teach us acceptance of what we cannot understand. Teach us understanding of what we cannot change. Deliver us from the futile questioning and second guessing which come with the words, "if only." For our life, Father, is in your good hands. You give life, and sustain life, and grant eternal life. You, and you alone, know us individually in our depths. Keep us who sob our grief in the hand of your Son who saves us, and so holds John before your throne. We thank you, our Father, even through clouded eyes, that through your Son, another son lives in the eternity of your House. Amen.

Text: Romans 7:21-8:2
So I find it to be a law that when I want to do right, evil lies close at hand. For I delight in the law of God, in my inmost self, but I see in my members another law at war with the law of my mind and making me captive to the law of sin which dwells in my members. Wretched man that I am, who will deliver me from this body of death? Thanks be to God through Jesus Christ our Lord! So then, I of myself serve the law of God with my mind, but with my flesh I serve the law of sin. . . . There is therefore now no condemnation for those who are in Jesus Christ.

This is a difficult time. These are difficult moments for many of us. For Pat, Sue, John, Michael, family, friends. It is a difficult time for me. I am filled, overwhelmed, with an aching sadness. And if I break apart at times, I hope you will understand. For John was my very best friend. He was more than a parishioner of Holy Trinity. He was my friend. I was more than his pastor. I was his friend.
Together, many of us ache today. But if this day, and these times, are going to have any meaning for our sadness in that big question of "why," then somehow, I've got to give it meaning and explanation from what is said here, for all of us.
Our Lord, in his earthly ministry, spoke in parables. This day, I would relate to you a modern-day parable, a story, which is true.
Once upon a time, there was a young man who was called to become the executive director of a small corporation. Over the years, he worked hard at his job, and the corporation grew, and the stockholders became many.

The day finally came when the Board of Directors decided the plant and facility of the corporation needed expansion. The executive director worked day and night to raise the capital, to serve the stockholders, and to carry on the business. It was an exhausting job for the executive director. He was torn in many directions, making many decisions in the early hours of the morning, as he tossed in his bed.

Finally, the day came to open the bids for the building expansion of the corporation. There was not enough capital. The expansion program exceeded the debt limit. The work of expansion had to begin all over again.

Tremendous pressure fell on the shoulders of the executive director. He could envision the corporation falling apart, just as he felt himself falling apart. The stocksholders had invested in good faith. They were unhappy. And the executive director began to hear of their unhappiness. He took everything that was said personally, until, hammered into the ground, he thought of himself as a failure. He even thought of resigning.

In the meantime, his personal life, away from the corporation, was disintegrating. The corporation did not pay him enough to care for his family. His personal financial problems loomed large, until everything piled up deeper and deeper and deeper, suffocating him.

Depression set in. He could not eat. He could not sleep, and he sank lower and lower, until he felt himself all alone.

The executive director was a man of faith, but even God became unreal. The wolves howled in the depths, and in the cellars of his mind. Even his friends, he felt, could not understand. Nor even those whom he loved the most, and who loved him the most. Even his wife. Only depression. Loneliness. Failure. Defeat. Broken pride. Not only to others, but to himself. It was only years later that he could admit to his wife that he had stopped at a gun shop, during those dark days, and had looked at the merchandise.

He began coming home from work early in the day, crawling into bed, attempting to escape in sleep. Depression, loneliness, howling wolves in his soul. God unreal. Escape from life; somehow, some way.

He would lie in bed curled into a fetal ball, shivering. Even there, and in that condition, the corporation and stockholders would not leave him alone. One even walked right into his house, into his bedroom, and shook him saying, "You've got to get up immediately." But the executive director was in no condition to make decisions, for in the hellish depths of his depression, he was beyond caring for anything: his business, his family, even himself.

He went through life in a trance. One day he came home early again from the job. Something was wrong with him, but he knew not what. He crawled into bed. Curled into a ball. Shivered again. And suddenly, that which he was feeling, made horrible, fearful sense. He knew he was on the brink of losing touch with reality. His mind began snapping back and forth like a rubber band. For two hours, his mind wavered back and forth between reality and the beyond. He knew exactly when he was in reality and he was rational, and he knew the times when his mind had snapped. It was sheer hell for him, for he knew from his depths that unreality was real!

Back and forth he wavered. Traveling a thin, red line. On the brink, on the edge of sanity, on the brink of snapping.

And if you've ever been there yourself, you have known hell, and what it means to feel abandoned, truly alone. Beyond reason, beyond rationality, beyond life as we know it. A thin, red line. Cross over it, and you are truly gone.

That is the parable.

When our Lord told a difficult story, he would explain it to his listeners. I would explain this true story to you.

The corporation is this church. The expansion program was the building and construction of this half-million dollar edifice. The stockholders were the congregation, and the executive director was its pastor.

Yes, the parable was about me. Depressed, alone, beyond the reach and touch of anyone. Almost losing complete touch with all reality.

Because I have been there, at that point of that hell, and because I knew John so well, I know what happened to him. I hope, that through my little true story, you, too, may know what happened to him.

I tell it, because I want you to realize that the John we each knew in our own ways did not take his own life. When that occurred, the John we knew, and the John who knew himself, no longer existed. And there are none of us who could have predicted it or who could have prevented it. For none of us knows the time, the place, the circumstances, the pressure points at which even we ourselve will snap, or knows what it will take. None of us knows himself so well, so completely. And we are filled today with an aching sadness, because unless we have been there ourselves, we cannot truly understand.

St. Paul, in our text read to you earlier, is speaking of just this area in his own way. Our inability to understand ourselves, and act accordingly. "When I want to do right," he says, "I find I cannot do it. And the evil I would never do, I somehow end up doing." "I am a wretched man," says Paul. "Who will deliver me from this body of death?" "Thanks be," he says, "to God, who gives us victory through Christ our Lord. There is therefore no condemnation for those who are in Christ Jesus."

Though we are aching and sorrowing today, there is no condemnation for John, who was in Christ Jesus his Lord. John has more life today than any of us who are remaining here in this body. What more can any of us say than that? What more can be said.

John is not here; he lives in the House of his Father. The Father who knows him, and he knows us, better than we know ourselves. He lives in the House of a Father who understands, and met him, and meets us where we are, in any condition we are in. He accepts us even when we cannot accept ourselves. For you see, God came to us, even before we could come to him. He came to us in Christ, and reconciled us to himself.

And though this is a day of sadness and mourning for us, it is not a day of sadness for those who precede us. For death holds no victory over them, or over us. Because Christ's tomb was empty, it proclaims to us that we will never be empty again. And though God may not answer our "whys," he is always present to fill the emptiness of our question marks.

For we can live in this life, even in deepest sorrow and tragedy when there is eternal hope. And eternal hope is so clearly ours in Jesus Christ.

John is with Christ, in the Father's House. And even in our loneliness, heartache, sorrow, and emptiness, our Lord does not leave us without his presence. "Cast your burdens upon me, for I care for you," are his words.

God does not forsake us, or leave us empty. He sent his Son to redeem our grief, and give us the Father's peace which passes even our human understanding of it. God is with us in our grief.

To you others, friends and relatives alike, you who are God's people as well, may God lead you to help and comfort these who mourn with your acts of love, kindness, understanding, and service. For God has called each of you to be the instruments of his love as we minister to one another. And may we all be found in Christ Jesus who redeems our grief by emptying himself upon the cross, in order that we might be full.

WE CANNOT JUDGE
Edward R. Mangelsdorf

Preached at the funeral of a sixty-two year old man who, when told he had terminal cancer, determined that he did not want to become a burden to his family, so took a shotgun and killed himself.

†††

A group of young men sit cowering in a
    muddy fox-hole in Vietnam — and suddenly,
    Someone yells, "Grenade."
One man throws himself upon it,
    absorbing the blast with his own body.
    He has lost his life for others.

A daughter, middle aged, sits staring out of
    a lonely window.
        She is unmarried, having given her whole
        life caring for an invalid mother.
    The years have passed her by, leaving a
    common and ordinary life.
She has given her life for another, but in a
    different way.

The figure of a man
    hangs limply from a cross, on a desolate
        hillside in Galilee, 2,000 years ago.
The crowd jeers, and spits in his face —
    and in the midst of these jeers, he
    cries out in great pain:
        "Father, forgive them — for they know not
    what they do."

Who knows what kinds of sacrifices have been
    made for us?
Who's to judge?

And who can say what any man's motivations are?
    What is it that makes a hero or a martyr?
        And what is that thin line that separates
        selfishness from godliness?

Thomas a Becket, the English priest and martyr,
    was praying in the Cathedral just before he
        was martyred — and he prayed:
            "O God, let me live for thee, and die for
            thee."

And, then Becket reflected:
    "Maybe I desire to die a martyr's death,
    not for the glory of God — but for the
        glory of self!"
Not even the saints could judge themselves.

I know not what motivates men to do any deed —
    No human being can judge, weigh, or sift
        another's motivations.
And we can't know — because we're not supposed
    to know.
Judgment is left to the Province of Almighty
    God.

But there is one thing we all do know —
    what we *should* do: and this we see set
        forth clearly in the life of Jesus Christ —
Not judgment, but compassion, charity, and
    understanding.

If we know this, then we know something of God,
    and his purpose for us.
We know that he is a loving and gracious God —
    Present where there is great hurt and pain;
    Present when people are bereaved and in
        distress;
    Present where there is any cross — and every
    cross — taking upon himself the suffering
        and pain of the world, bearing the burden
        too heavy for any one man.

And we know of this gracious God through the Church,
    that recalls the words of the psalmist:
"The Lord will preserve your going out and
    coming in from this time forth and forever
    more."

God is a loving and merciful Father, who will
    keep, protect, and preserve his children in
    this life and in life to come.
No guarantee against disease, sickness, or
    bodily death.
No grandiose visions of a life without trials
    and tribulations —
    But a firm confidence in a loving God, who
    will always be with us.

And, again, this same confidence, expressed by
        him, nailed to a cross, against the
        pale Galilean sky:
"Father, into thy hands, I commit my spirit."

That faith in God's love was uttered 3,000 years
    ago by the psalmist.
        2,000 years ago by Our Lord himself, and now,
            this day, by those of us who have gathered
                together —
Not only to grieve over our separation, but
    to confess our faith in that very same love
        of God.

That same love of God that manifested itself
    on Easter morning,
        when Christ broke the bands of death, and
            arose to proclaim God's eternal and immortal life to
            all men.

That same message of love that the church
    proclaims this day:
        "There is no death — only Life.
        Look to Jesus Christ — the Face of God."

We come to grieve — and to celebrate.
    To grieve at our own loss —
        and to celebrate the love of God, in whom
            there is no death.

Death is not glorious and wonderful:
    It is painful and heartbreaking for us who
        stand here this day.
But neither is life glorious and wonderful —
    It, too, is painful and heartbreaking — as
        mature people know.

Faith in God's love, and God's Resurrected Life
    doesn't make life any easier:
Rather, it adds one quality to life which would
    be missing without the resurrection:
        Hope.

The Hope that drove a tiny band of frightened
    disciples to proclaim God's love in the Risen Lord
        to the world.
The Hope that makes life bearable in the midst
    of great pain, suffering, and loss.
The Hope that bears all things in the face of
    death — our own, and others.

A soldier, a daughter, and Our Lord Jesus Christ.
    Sacrifices that confront us daily:
        some are noticed, some slip quietly by,
            and some are celebrated for eternity.

We *don't* know what motivates men and women
  to do what they do — but this is not our
  province.
We are not here to judge, but to share.
  Not here to pass God's judgment, but to be
  compassionate.
As children of God, we know what we *are* to do:
  The watchwords of God's people are
    love, joy, confidence — trust, hope,
    and sharing.

The confidence of a psalmist, the confidence of
  Christ, our confidence ringing out this
  day, as we confess a God of mercy and
  understanding, and love.

If you had a child, and that child hurt himself,
    either accidentally or even deliberately —
  You would gather him to yourself — and take
    that great pain upon yourself, giving
    comfort, love, and understanding.
If so, how much more does our Father in Heaven,
  enfold all of us who suffer and grieve,
    who labor under the burden of great pain
    and depression?

And who is this Comforter we are sent, if not
  the Holy Spirit of the Living God himself?
  Who is to comfort, never ceasing to
    comfort?

This day, we reaffirm our faith in our Loving
    Father, and say with Our Lord Jesus Christ,
  "Father, into Thy hands we commend this
    soul — and our souls — for healing,
    and mercy, and comfort."

For thou art a Loving God who will preserve
  our going out and coming in, from this
    time forth, and evermore, world without
    end. Amen.

Funeral Sermons for Persons Stricken Suddenly

AS WE LOOK TO THE MOUNTAIN
James D. Schmidt

Preached at the community memorial service for a minister in his sixties, who died suddenly, of a heart attack, just prior to the opening of an annual cooperative venture among several churches.

†††

As I look around the sanctuary this evening, I am struck by the many different ways that our lives have been touched by the life of The Reverend Richard F. Wilcox. We have known him as a loving son and brother who stepped into his father's shoes at an early age, temporarily giving up his own hopes and goals for the future to help keep his family together and going. We have known him as a devoted husband and father, bringing joy and vision and a zest for life, in all of its richness, into his own family unit. We have known him as a dedicated pastor, preaching the Word of God to his congregation not only from this pulpit, but also through his loving presence at the hospital, across the counseling table, in the home, and at special times of joy and grief. We have known him as a trusted colleague, active in the life of his denomination and, at the same time, thoroughly committed to the ecumenical movement as expressed through that special bond of fellowship which exists among the churches here in Champion and through the Warren Area Clergy Association. We have known him as a valued friend and neighbor. And we have come together tonight to blend all of our varied experiences with Dick into a joyous song of thanksgiving to God for permitting us to share in his life and in his faith.

Certainly, there is sorrow and grief among us tonight, and we shed our tears without shame, for our loss is a real one and a personal one. But, God has not left us comfortless. God has visited us once again tonight with power in his holy Word; and, in his word from Scripture, we are invited to share in that which motivated Dick's life as a servant of Jesus Christ.

Psalm 121 was a special favorite of Dick and Virginia's, and for the next few moments, I would like to share some reflections upon it with you. This Psalm was originally one of the songs sung by pilgrims in ancient Israel as they made their way to Jerusalem for the celebration of major festival days. Jesus most probably knew this Psalm and sang it himself when he went up to Jerusalem. For many people, it was a long pilgrimage up to Jerusalem — one in which they were often forced to camp in the desert along the way. And the psalmist sees in their journey a parable of our own pilgrimages through life. He pictures himself looking toward the neighboring mountains where sentries would have been posted in the evening to protect the people against the sudden attacks of wandering bands of robbers. As he looks, he sees the sentries in place, but even more, beyond them he sees another guardian, the Lord himself. And this sentry never slumbers or sleeps in the lovingkindness that he has for all of his children. And so the psalmist can lie down to be refreshed by sleep, confident that the Lord will keep him safe from all danger . . . that the Lord will protect us as we come in and go out, from now on and forever.

What wonderful words of comfort and hope belong to us through this Psalm! Is it any wonder that the apostle Paul could build upon these words in the triumphant shout that concludes the eighth chapter of his letter to the church at Rome: "I am convinced," he wrote there, "that nothing can separate us from the love of God — neither death nor life, neither angels nor other heavenly rulers or powers, neither the present nor the future, neither the world above nor the world below — there is nothing in all of creation that will ever be able to separate us from the love of God which is ours through Christ Jesus, our Lord."

We have all heard these words before, but I think that it is important for us to hear them again tonight. For you see, the hopes and the dreams and the love and the faith that we have shared with Dick are not in vain. We have this treasure in our human vessels, given us by God. And even though our vessels become battered and bruised and finally broken through life's pilgrimage, we still have this treasure given us by God himself, and the Word of our God will live forever.

And so we look to the mountains tonight, and we know that our help and our hope also come from the Lord who made heaven and earth. We pause, each in his or her own way, giving thanks for the victory which leads to eternal life that God has given us in Jesus Christ. And we give him thanks for sharing his life with us through faithful servants like Richard Wilcox.

How well we can close our meditation tonight with the ancient words of thanksgiving found in the Nunc Dimittis: "Lord, let your servant depart now in peace, according to your word: for our eyes have seen your salvation, which you have prepared before the face of all people; a light to lighten the gentiles and the glory of your people Israel."

Glory to the Father, and to the Son, and to the Holy Spirit, both now and forevermore!

"WHY ARE YOU CAST DOWN, O MY SOUL?"
Kieth Gerberding

Preached upon the sudden death of a husband, aged sixty-one.

†††

Why are you cast down, O my soul, and why are you disquieted within me? Hope in God; for I shall again praise him, my help and my God. (Psalm 42:11)

Now our souls are cast down. This unexpected tragedy has upset us. Our hearts are "disquieted" within us.

You, dear sister, have become burdened with a heavy load of sorrow. Your soul is cast down. You wanted to grow old together with your husband. You were looking forward to living many more years of good life together. You desired to continue your days of living with God, in his church. Now this has changed. Our arms of sympathy and concern reach out to you today, feeling the hurt and agony that afflicts you.

Yet there is something today which has not changed. What has occurred has certainly not erased your hope, so firmly grounded in God's love. On this day, you have faith to hope for reunion with your husband, because our Lord has conquered death. He lives forever that we might all live forever with him.

You also hope to continue to please God in your life now, as you find ways to work, serve, and help others in his name. And you hope to have your heart raised again in joy. On new mornings, the sunshine of hope and happiness in Christ will once again flood your life.

"I shall again praise him." Our Father in heaven knows us well. He can accept the fact that there are times when we have difficulty singing a song of joy. He really cares about what is happening in our lives. His love is focused on us now, in this time of sorrow.

He looks at us now and says, "All right. My peace I give to you." In the days to come you will again praise him. His love for you is constant in Christ. Already now we sense his kindness surrounding us.

God is our help! He is the One who lifts us through sorrow and pain. He does not leave us without comfort in our time of anguish. Perhaps not all of our questions are answered. We are disquieted by thoughts of our own failure to do as much as we might have for the one who has now been taken from us. We wish we could explain, and justify all things. God our loving Father says to each of us, "Peace." He forgives our failures, and gives us new strength for days of love and service. He will enable us to live for him and for others.

Be consoled with this assurance. God is "Our Father" today and forever. Through Jesus Christ we will again praise him, our help and our God.

HE WHO KEEPS YOU
Lawrence Ruegg

*Preached at the double funeral for a man and his wife, in their early
sixties, who were killed in the crash of a small aircraft of which the
husband was pilot.*

†††

The world around us increases in modernization. There are new ways
to get to new places to do new things. It is inevitable that we be caught
up in this whirlwind of progress. Yet, it is also determined that we — as
creatures of this earth — do not really change that much. We still possess
the ancient human need for love, comfort, hope, and meaning. I don't
know about each of you, but I find that as I grow older — even as I
experience the newness of the world's progress; even as I see and do and
enjoy the advantages of today's life; even in the midst of that — I find
myself reverting inwardly to the past. As I become older I find the
greatest comfort and meaning for life expressed by ancient shepherds. I
discover my feelings encased in the beautiful words of Old Testament
Psalms.

There is something about the psalmists' attitudes and language that
is akin to our own thoughts. There is something about their hopes that
speaks to our own wishes. There is something timeless about what they
said, something that speaks to the unchangeable part within us. As we
grow older, we relearn from their words what they had known about life
and about God.

The Psalms are most often used at Christian burials. I suppose it is
because it assumed that the psalmists were speaking about death: "Yea,
though I walk through the valley of the shadow of death, I will fear no
evil, for Thou art with me; Thy rod and Thy staff, they comfort me." I
had always read that with a view toward the time when I would leave
this earth in the death of my body. More recently, however, I view it as
words of assurance during my lifetime, as I must face the death of
others: my family, my friends, my parishoners.

Today is one of those "valleys of the shadow of death." Today is a
time when we might share the feelings of a living shepherd as he once
had to bury the bodies of those he loved. This is the time of which the
23rd Psalm speaks to me: not our own death, but the death of those we
love. "The shadow of death" has suddenly — instantaneously — moved
across the experience of this family. A darkness has quickly blotted out
joy and dreams and relationships.

In the many times that such events happen to us, the modernization
of this world has nothing to offer us for comfort. Whether we work in
high rise office buildings or on the ancient meadows of Palestine, the
human question is the same — the psalmist has merely written it first: "I
lift up my eyes to the hills. From whence does my help come?"

The psalmist has learned that true help does not come from the hills.

True comfort and hope and strength does not come from what this earth has to offer. Oh, there are things of this creation that might soften the blow and sedate us for awhile. Friendship can do that. Human compassion serves its purpose to assist us to accept what now is. But, the only real and lasting help comes from him who is beyond the hills of this planet. That was what the psalmist had learned through experience. "My help comes from the Lord who made heaven and earth." That is the witness which he gives us. That is the good news of the love and salvation which God has to offer. Though you must now walk through this valley of the shadow of death — though you must now walk it in grief, in separateness, with tears, with longings — yet, the promise of God is that you need fear no evil for God is with you with comfort.

There is comfort in the knowledge that we bury only bodies. The spirits which once lived there are secure in the arms of their Lord. Their eternal life is guaranteed by the blood of Jesus Christ. To him we commend them, reminding our Lord of his promise to save all who believe in him. Death is never a pleasant time to face. But it is bearable in the face of the hope that is our gift from God: the hope that we know in the resurrection of Jesus Christ.

There is also comfort in the knowledge of God's forgiveness of us. The wrong that we may have done toward those whose bodies were killed, and the good toward them that we neglected to do — that is all behind us now; and God forgives what money and grief cannot buy. That's the good news of God: forgiveness. It has not changed with any modernization. As it was real to the psalmists, let it be real for you.

There is also comfort for the future in the knowledge that our God walks with us in good times and bad: " . . . he who keeps you will not slumber nor sleep . . . The Lord will keep your going out and your coming in, from this time forth and for evermore." That is the hope with which the psalmist faced the difficult tomorrow. That is the hope which has been realized by countless Christians down through the centuries. It is because people of God have trusted God and found him faithful that we have preserved for us the words of faith we heard tonight.

May God grant such hope and faith to you. May the God of Abraham, the God of King David, the God of St. Paul, and the God of (names) bring you comfort today and strength for tomorrow. "My help comes from the Lord who made heaven and earth. Surely goodness and mercy shall follow me all the days of my life, and I will dwell in the house of the Lord forever."

ALWAYS BE PREPARED
Carroll R. Gunkel

Preached upon the sudden death of a man who was victim of a heart attack.

††††

Text: Matthew 22:2-14

Jesus told a parable — a very strange parable — about a king who prepared a wedding feast for his son. It was to be a time of great gaiety. Invitations were extended to a great number of people. The anticipated joy was soon dampened, however, as people sent word back that, for one reason or another, they could not attend.

There were crops to be planted, merchandise to be sold, sick to be tended — many obligations which made it impossible to accept the invitation to the wedding feast.

The king was exceedingly distraught — even to the point of anger and ultimately to the point of desperation. After all, what is a party without the guests? It seemed as though there were to be no guests.

To remedy this unpleasant situation, the host ordered his servants to go out into the streets and invite everyone they met to come to the wedding feast. Strangers were better than no guests at all.

This procedure seemed to be producing the desired results until the servants met a man who refused their invitation, protesting that he was not properly dressed. Perhaps he was a working man on his way home from a particularly trying day. Perhaps there was some other reason why he was unkempt — whatever the cause, he was obviously not in any condition to attend a wedding. Despite his protests, the king's servants insisted he come to the wedding. With great reluctance, he did as he was told.

One can hardly account for what happened next in this amazing parable. According to Jesus' words, when the king entered the banquet hall and his gaze fell on this one disheveled guest, his anger became greater than when it first became obvious that his son's wedding feast was not going to be all he had anticipated.

In a great rage, the host demanded an explanation, only to be told by his servants that they were only obeying his orders. Countermanding his earlier directions, he now ordered the servants to bind the hapless man and cast him out of the house.

This they did, producing an intriguing question.

What was Jesus saying?

He was saying what we need to hear in this moment.

He was saying that everyone of us should be prepared for any eventuality. Most especially, we should all so live that, should God call us to leave this life for life with him, we would be prepared to respond.

The necessity of such preparation becomes obvious when one stands in the face of death — particularly sudden death.

With suddeness — like a thief in the night the New Testament says — death comes.

No one of us can ever anticipate the moment or the circumstance when death shall overtake us. What we can anticipate is the necessity for living well every moment so that, whenever death does come, it will find us being faithful to the gospel of Jesus Christ.

In the case of our brother in Christ whom we now memorialize, it was a heart attack — striking so suddenly that there was not even a moment in which to cry out.

The act of death could have come just as suddenly through accident or stroke. The manner of dying is not nearly so important as the manner of living.

How would death find us:

angry at some slight — supposed or real, or forgiving as we expect to be forgiven;

bitter because others have so much more materially than we do or thankful for what we do have;

sullen because we have not gotten "our way" about something; or rejoicing that we can grow by *not* always getting what we want;

morose because the day has been gray when we wanted to have sunshine; or elated because the sun still shines someplace and will shine for us again;

depressed because illness has limited us or those whom we love; or praising God for the abundant gift we have received;

caught in the web of our sinful actions; or seeking forgiveness for our past sins and fortitude to resist future failures?

How shall death find us?

This is the question with which Jesus was dealing in this parable. We should always so live the good life of the gospel, that even though death could catch us unawares physically, death could never catch us unprepared spiritually.

Whenever death shall come, Jesus suggests, we should be found living so faithfully the precepts of the gospel that there shall be no question but that we shall be able to enter into the wedding feast of eternity and shall not be found wanting.

THE VICTORY
Robert S. Kinsey

Preached upon the death of a man, age sixty-five, who was victim of a heart attack.

†††

On that first Easter morning, three women were hurrying through the dark, narrow streets of Jerusalem. According to God's plan on that first Easter, the sun was destined to rise on the greatest day in history. No, the women did not carry brightly colored pocketbooks on that first Easter, nor did they wear bright colors. Weren't they in mourning? Didn't they have a sad and solemn duty to perform? They were not hurrying to greet a Risen Savior; they were going to anoint a corpse, a corpse buried in a borrowed tomb on Good Friday. One question dominated their thinking — "Who will roll away the stone from the entrance to the grave for us?" (Mark 16:3) You know the outcome of this event which began in sorrow and ended in joy. The stone was rolled away. There was no corpse to anoint. They listened to the greatest — and probably the shortest — Easter sermon ever preached. A sermon preached not by a seminary graduate but by an angel from the eternal heavens: "Don't be alarmed," he said. "You are looking for Jesus of Nazareth who was nailed to the cross. But he is not here — he has risen! Look, here is the place where they laid him . . . "

You and I love and worship and serve the Risen Lord. Because he lives, our loved ones shall live. He has overcome sin, death, and the grave. Wasn't the first item on the agenda of the early church to proclaim the resurrection of God's Son? Up and down the Mediterranean world they went, not with a Bible under their arms, but with the message of the Risen Savior in their hearts and on their lips. *Jesus Christ is alive.* He lives and reigns for all eternity. Because he lives, you and I shall live, and our loved ones whom we give over to his care will live!

To you, Bev, Barb, Gene, and the rest of the family, I say . . . remember! Remember that death does not have the last word. No one can deny that death is an enemy. Doesn't God's book describe death as the last enemy to be overcome? (1 Corinthians 15:26) Remember, though, that death does not have the last word: the Word Incarnate has the final word, a word of victory and hope!

Today we honor the memory of Marshall E. Leiter, a father, brother, grandfather, and a friend . . . a faithful member of Trinity Church. Recently Marshall returned to Ashland and joined again the church where his parents were so faithful and where Marshall had been baptized and confirmed by Dr. Arthur Smith. Marshall planned to come to one of the Holy Communion services last Sunday. Doesn't Holy Communion foreshadow that Messianic banquet in heaven when our Lord himself will be the host? In faith, we know that Marshall will be a guest at that banquet.

As we sit here in the presence of death, what do we learn? Life is short. Didn't Job say, "My days were swifter than a runner"? (Job 9:25) If Job were living today, he would probably say, "My days are swifter than a jet." Since life is short, shouldn't the prayer of the psalmist be on our lips, too: "So teach us to number our days that we may apply our hearts unto wisdom." (Psalms 90:12)

Marshall's death makes that other world even more real. Wasn't Henry Ward Beecher trying to express the same thought when he said, "Tears are often the telescope through which men see far into heaven."

As a family, a time like this will bring you even closer together in your common sorrow. As you comfort each other and as you meditate on the ultimate issues of life, you will be inspired to minister to others who walk through the valley of sorrows.

On that first Easter morning, the women were sure that they had a sad and solemn duty to perform. They did not anoint a corpse; they learned about a Risen Savior — your Savior and mine. In faith we commit Marshall into Christ's loving care. Together with Paul we sing the victory song: "Where, O Death is your victory? Where, O Death, is your power to hurt? . . . But thanks be to God who gives us the victory through our Lord Jesus Christ!" (1 Corinthians 15:55, 57)

TODAY IS THE DAY OF REPENTANCE: DON'T PROCRASTINATE!
Phillip B. Giessler

Preached upon the death of an elderly woman who, seemingly, was recovering nicely from a broken hip, when she was stricken by a heart attack.

†††

And so, as the Holy Spirit says, Today, if you hear Him speak, don't close your minds as it happened when the people provoked Me at the time they tested me in the desert, where your fathers put Me to a test when for forty years they saw what I could do. That was why I was angry with those people, and I said, "In their hearts they always wander around and never have learned My paths." So because I was angry I swore they will never come to My place of rest! See to it, fellow Christians, that none of you has a wicked, unbelieving heart that turns away from the living God. Yes, *encourage* one another every day, as long as you can say today, to keep sin from deceiving anyone of you with its pleasure and closing your mind to the truth. We share in Christ if we only keep our first confidence unshaken to the end. (Hebrews 3:7-14)

In the Name of Jesus, he who is the Resurrection and the Life, friends of our sister Helena, now fallen asleep, and especially you, the immediate family of a mother, grandmother, and sister now called home.

I.

Who would have guessed just a week ago that we would be here today? But God has arranged it for a purpose. No, that purpose is not to praise our departed Christian sister — though we shall say a few words about her strong faith in Jesus.

Certainly we must speak glory to Christ's Name as the One who has delivered Helena into heavenly mansions above.

But most of all, we gather to have a word spoken to ourselves in preparation of the time we are faced with death.

This means we come to a time of a funeral. Of such a time, J. R. Chiles writes, "Funerals at times can be so faithfully and so prayerfully conducted as to change the destiny of the living. Only that which is true, that which is right, that which is kind, and that which is helpful has any proper place in a funeral service. Faults of the dead are not to be minimized nor false hopes permitted for anybody. Christ is the only Saviour, repentance and faith the only way to get to Him, and the obedience of a spiritual life, the only proper testimony for Him. Ministers are asked to conduct funerals because they preach the word of truth and ought to do so something in line with the calling of God and the expectations of the people."*

Such a Word of Scripture we wish to communicate on the basis of an ancient text meant for our Twentieth Century lives. It deals with death and the danger of *procrastination.*

It says that TODAY is the day for repentance — for, within twenty-four hours, we may be called home as has been Helena.

Are you ready in honest confession of sin and true belief in Jesus?

If you aren't, you are procrastinating! And the only kind of procrastination which the Lord favors is the putting-off-of-sin, not the putting-off-of-belief.

But, since we cannot put off sins of ourselves, but have Christ who has taken them off of us by his death on the cross, we cannot procrastinate concerning *belief.*

That's why the writer of Hebrews says, "And so, as the Holy Spirit says, Today, if you hear him speak, don't close your minds as it happened when the people provoked me at the time they tested Me in the desert, where your fathers put me to a rest when for forty years they saw what I could do."

You can read that story of Israel's foolishness in the Old Testament book of *Numbers.* God passed the test but many Israelites flunked it into hell because they procrastinated — and their TODAYS became the TOMORROWS of death before they were ready.

They closed their minds to Yahweh's warnings and deliberately sinned.

Of it all, God said, "That is why I was angry with those people, and I said, 'In their hearts they always wander around and never have learned my paths.' So because I was angry I swore they will never come to my place of rest!"

And his warning to us is just as sharp. He says, in the text, "See to it, fellow Christians, that none of you has a wicked, unbelieving heart that turns away from the living God."

To heed that warning and pass the test before us calls for the word of *encouragement* in the next verse of the text from Hebrews. The writer says: "Yes, encourage one another every day, as long as you can say TODAY, to keep sin from deceiving any one of you with its pleasure and closing your mind to the truth."

Are any of you deceived at this moment? What are your sins? Does alcoholism have control of you or greed or gossip or laziness or just plain unbelief? Don't play the game of waiting with these sins TODAY. But, rather give those sins to Jesus in confession and take his offer of forgiveness and a new life TODAY before He comes TOMORROW — maybe even TODAY — in death.

Helena took the warning and encouragement many years ago. She knew the truth of the text's final words: "We share in Christ if we only keep our first confidence unshaken to the end."

---

*John R. Chiles, *A Treasure of Funeral Messages* (Grand Rapids: Baker Book House, 1966), p. 15.

II.

TODAY we are alive. God calls us in his mercy — and often calls longer than we deserve.

But don't tempt him. His patience runs out and death sets in. Yes, contrary to the thinking of many Twentieth Century personalities, God is a God of wrath as well as a God of love.

There is a hell for the procrastinator. The cross of Christ shows this. God would not have demanded the death of his Son if sin did not have to be paid for; he would not have forsaken Jesus if transgression could be passed by lightly. So it is that he who does not believe by the truth of Christ's cross is lost.

But the cross shows forgiveness, life, and heaven for those who repent TODAY. Christ's sacrifice destroyed the consequences of hell and you can have the blessings of that today.

Friends, picture a globe the size of our planet — eight thousand miles across made of solid granite. Suppose that a little bird flies to a certain spot only *once* each year and takes one peck. Year after year he pecks in the same spot. Then after one thousand years, a scratch appears on the surface. When that bird has the whole planet pecked away, then eternity will be over. But we know that it will not even be over then.

Do you wish to procrastinate with the chance of spending eternity in the wrong place, missing out on the glories of the heaven Helena has now inherited?

No wonder the Holy Ghost says, "TODAY (as) you hear (God) speak, don't close your minds . . . "

There will be no second chance. Scripture says, "It is appointed unto men once to die and then the judgment." (Hebrews 9:27) And again: "If a tree fall toward the south or toward the north, in the place where the tree falleth, there shall it be." (Ecclesiastes 11:3)

May you be ready for heaven TODAY. AMEN.

Funeral Sermons for the Young and Very Young

INTO HIS ARMS
George L. Bell

Preached at the funeral of a teenage boy who was killed in an accident.

✝✝✝

Texts employed: Romans 8; Revelation 7; John 14; Psalms 39, 35, 121, 23

What else can you do in a moment like this but say and show "I am with you." We are with you.

We cannot give the reason for this turn of events. We can only join in the human question of the moment. "My God, my God, why?" The question of agony comes from the lips of the Son of God on the cross into the hearts and minds of us all. "My God, why this life cut short?"

Why this family touched with tragedy?

Why must we walk the lonely path of separation now?

Why the accident?

There is no need to try to cover the sense of intense grief we have, the unbelieving shock we all know. For grief has its place in the human experience — and its bitter wine is something all must taste.

Certainly Job has set a model for human reaction which is worth remembering. In his sickness — his loss of family, cattle, property — he cried out to God in anger. He struggled to find an answer and found each word of counsel from friends absurdly irrelevant. He talked about the vacant, lonely feeling within — and the temptations he had to give up and attempt to try again. Yet he comes out of this dialogue with God with perhaps the most beautiful statement of faith to be found in the Bible. "I know my Redeemer liveth — and because he lives, I too shall live."

One reason I'm attracted to the Scriptures is because they fit life so well. They do not gloss over grief and say buck up and smile — everything is really all right — this is God's will. The Bible says, "It's okay to cry — to express all the human pain that is there. God can take your tears and your atomic bombs. And, if you'll hold on to him, he can turn your tragedy into something creative and good." And so we grow by something which would shatter the lives of others and thrust them into permanent bitterness.

So, I'm not here to stop the tears — or to say wise words to ease the pain. I'm here to secure your hand and mine in a firm handclasp with the God who spoke Mike into being and who gave us our lives. I know we were designed for such a divine-human partnership and now we need to acknowledge and celebrate that.

Yet this moment must be more than a moment to acknowledge grief. We must not let our grief get in the road of recounting the wonder and dignity of this life. While we did not have Mike long, he still was the bearer of gifts to each of us. Think of the gifts — a son bears to a father —

a son bears to a mother — to a brother and sisters — and to a special buddy — and friends. Think of his style of life — his special ways of saying things — the times when someone else has made you happy and proud to know him because of a compliment they paid him. Nineteen years he passed on his special brand of joy — and challenges — his special flavor of spice. No one ever can or will take his place. Each human makes and keeps his own place and, when he leaves life, whether by sickness, or by accident, or on a battlefield — he leaves a vacant spot in the pageant of life.

Now we count these gifts — and with each memory, we turn to God who loaned him to us for a while and we say, "thank you, God." Let us celebrate the sparkling treasure chest he placed in our lives!

We also pause now to reflect on the context in which his life — and ours, is set. There are within us and around us all kinds of clues which lead us to sense and to believe that, while we are human, we are more than human. We are not dust that returns to dust, earth that returns to earth. We are more. Something in us whispers that we are designed for an eternity.

We feel a kinship with a butterfly that leaves behind the cocoon. We sense we are like a seed, which must die when planted in the ground before it can take on the new body of a plant which will bear fruit, or a blossom. There is an automatic sensing within that, though we may know the realities of the night, we will also know the wonder and beauty of the sunrise.

The Bible encourages us to dream and increases our expectation. "Your dreams cannot reach too far. You can't even come close to the wonderful reality God has in store after death. Mansions — no night or day — no fears — no pain — no sickness — fellowship — trust — love — unbelievable. All gifts of God who loved you the moment you were conceived — loved you every moment of every day — and surrounds you with his blanket of love in the moments of your death. God was with Mike in those quiet moments in his room — loving him through his experience of separation — and God's love fills him now as he is in his beyond.

And so it is with us. We cannot know the tons of love he is pouring into this room — into our hearts — and lives. He's here, too — meeting us — giving dignity to our human lot and promising to take even this pain and transform it into hope.

Some are broken by tragedy — never to be repaired. Some grow because of tragedy into unexpected — new — beautiful ways. The difference? Some accept — others reject the gifts only God himself can give. Let us open our lives to receive his love and gently and trustingly lay Mike in the loving arms of our God — his God.

GOD'S WONDERFUL PLANS
Frank L. Starkey

Preached at the funeral of a young man, age twenty-one, who had made two tours in Vietnam and, after discharge, met with a motorcycle accident a few miles from home when attempting to miss an oncoming car.

†††

Sometimes death comes suddenly and unexpectedly. In the midst of life, with every joy of living near at hand, the one we love is taken from us. The tragic events of life remind us of the truth of those words uttered by the young man, David, long ago ... Death is, indeed, but a step away.

We are grateful for the life of our son in the faith, Duane. He just returned, not many weeks ago, from serving our country in Vietnam, there in our behalf, to help insure the freedom that we hold as a Christian principle, for all people. He served for you and me, for God and country.

That makes it doubly hard for us to see such a tragic event happen here in the safety of our own land and community. And yet, this, too, is a fact of life that we must face. How shall we understand it?

To do so, we must review some of the basic tenets of our Christian faith. God has created us out of love. And such a love, which we aren't really able to understand, carries with it certain dangers. Because God loves us, he must allow certain freedoms to operate. He must give us the chance to respond out of free choice to all we do. He refuses to make us behave in any certain, given way. We must be able to reject him as well as accept his love and care.

That means that he must then create all things with that in mind. And so he created certain basic laws to govern his creation, laws which make all sorts of mistakes and dangers possible, mistakes in good judgment, evil intentions, and the hazard of the other people around us as well.

And so it is, in that kind of an atmosphere, he shows us his love, and gives us an opportunity to grow in a real joyous way.

But then you see how all sorts of misfortunes and evils can happen, too. Tragedies are possible every moment of every day. And so David said so very wisely, death is but a step away from any of us.

And yet, what a joy it is to know a good son. That is part of our created freedom, too. God has given us the joy of sharing in his creation through the giving of life to a son. He has given us the joy of watching that personality grow, of giving of our love to him, of sacrificing for his good, of knowing the same kind of a relationship with our child as God has with us. As we go through the joys and sorrows of helping our children to grow, so God goes through the joys and sorrows of helping us to grow, in freedom; freedom to accept or reject his love.

If we were to leave our analysis here, it would be only selfish, for certainly our sorrow is for our own personal loss, and that's all right, too. It's right that we should know that personal sorrow.

But the overwhelming truth of the matter is that such a God, who is so great a God to allow all the freedoms he does, and to give us such a marvelous gift of life that he has, such a God does not leave us out in the cold because of tragedy. He has built into us the desire to preserve life with every ounce of know-how that he gives us; but, knowing how great our God is, we also know that, through the tragedies of life, he will never for a moment forsake us, or our loved one. We can rest assured that he sees us through the valley of the shadow of death.

And all we have to do is look at all the things he has told us in his marvelous Word. Everything he did while he was here on this earth speaks to us of the assurance of the truth that we believe in. This is why we say Jesus was the Way, the Truth, and the Life. He didn't tell us about it; he demonstrated it always. He demonstrated his power over nature, mind, and body. He sealed it with his own resurrection. And he promised he would always be with us to be our source of strength.

And that power is still a reality for us today. Our experience of tragedy and loss is still the same. Our tears flow just as easily even after knowing this. But the Christ is still with us, and we face the time of sorrow in the strength that we receive from faith in him.

There are only three incidents recorded in the Scriptures of Jesus raising someone from the dead. Jesus couldn't go around doing this all the time. In fact, all these did finally die again. But you see the whole purpose was to tell us the truth of the fact that he is God; and God is love; so he created; and he will raise us again as he has promised. He overcomes our grief, for he reminds us that death is not an ending to existence but rather the beginning of a new kind of life. "Eye hath not seen, ear hath not heard, what wonderful things God has planned for those who love him."

CAN WE GIVE THANKS?
Carl B. Rife

Preached upon the death of a boy, age six, who was born with a palsied condition which inhibited his physical and mental growth and made him extremely susceptible to illness. He died when his body could no longer resist the latest illness.

†††

Rejoice always, pray constantly, give thanks in all circumstances; for this is the will of God in Jesus Christ for you. (1 Thessalonians 5:17-18)

Give thanks in all circumstances? Can we give thanks when death, death to one so precious and dear to us, has visted our home?

The testimony of Scripture and the experience of countless Christians down through the ages answer yes to this question.

There is the experience of the Pilgrims. They gave thanks in the midst of their hardships, in the mist of much suffering and death. For, although they did not understand in every detail what their ordeal meant, they in faith saw the hand of God at work in their midst, bringing good out of evil, life out of death.

Can *we* give thanks?

I. Yes, we can give thanks because God has shared the life of Timmy with us.

When a child is born, we experience his birth, his coming into our midst as a gift of God. But sometimes we, as parents, forget our initial feelings and start thinking that the child belongs to us. The death of a child reminds all of us that the life of our child — of all children, indeed of all persons — belongs to God. But even more, we are reminded that any life *is a gift shared with us by God*, be it for six years or sixty.

By your own testimony, Gloria and Aaron, you have understood this truth. You have said many times that Timmy truly was a gift of God. He has brought dimensions of life and understanding to your family beyond measure and understanding.

And, as family and friends, the rest of us have experienced this gift through you and your family, through your quiet but eloquent faith and witness. We have gotten a glimpse of what God had in mind when he blessed your family with Timmy.

II. We can give thanks because God has promised us a richer and fuller life beyond this life.

The most comforting truth of this hour is that Timmy is in God's loving care. Remember Jesus' words: "Let the children come to me, do not hinder them; for to such belongs the kingdom of God."

Timmy has gone before us to that dimension of life where suffering and pain will be relieved, where broken lives will be made whole, where tears will be wiped away.

I am overjoyed to know a God who reveals himself in a person who said, "See that you do not despise one of these little ones; for I tell you that in heaven their angels always behold the face of my Father who is in heaven."

III. We can give thanks because God comforts us in our loneliness, loss and sorrow.

He alone can fill the emptiness left in our lives by the loss of a son, a brother.

Here the Scriptures speak most eloquently to us in our need.

"The Lord is my shepherd, I shall not want . . . "

"Let not your heart be troubled."

"Underneath are the everlasting arms."

"For I am persuaded that neither death, nor life, nor angels, nor principalities, nor powers, nor things present, nor things to come, nor height, nor depth, nor any other creature, shall be able to separate us from the love of God, which is in Christ Jesus, our Lord."

The same God who shared Timmy with you, who embraces Timmy in his everlasting arms will comfort you in your time of loss and sorrow.

Can we give thanks? Yes, by the grace of God we can and we do.

GOD SUFFERS WITH US
Michael L. Sherer

Preached upon the untimely death of someone young.

✝✝✝

. . . so then, whether we live or whether we die, we are the Lord's. (Romans 14:8b)

Who can understand the death of someone young? What meaning can there be in that? Why should it happen?

It might be a simple thing for a pastor merely to say that such an event is the will of God, which, of course, we do not understand. I will not say that to you today, because it has never been easy to know clearly what the will of God is in specific events. Often God simply does not tell us. It is true that many times things happen which we do not like and which we do *not* think to be the will of God, which actually are. But it is also true that men often call events the will of God which simply are not. God has given us some broad clues about what his will is for us. But it is clear that many things happen in our world which are *not* God's will. God is not happy about sin. He does not rejoice when wars break out. He certainly does not cause them. Neither is God pleased with quarreling and fighting between people, nor divorce, nor dishonesty in the world. But these things continue to happen. There is no doubt that many things happen which are not according to God's will.

Perhaps that part is not so difficult to understand. We can agree, perhaps, that God gives men the freedom to do good or evil so that there may be choice and meaning in life. But why does he permit the death, for example, of a small child, who does not even understand evil yet? What kind of God is *that?* Or what kind of God sits idly by while tragedy — the unfairest kind — takes it toll? What kind of God is *that?*

I would suggest to you that a *loving* God permits such things. But I must use an illustration. Suppose there is a father who loves his young son very much. As the boy grows older the father looks after him and provides all the lad needs for a healthy life. But, as the boy grows older, his father must make an important decision. Should he try to give complete protection to his son that no harm or evil ever comes his way, or should he free his son to experience even risky things in the world, so that the boy may learn to be responsible, able to make choices, able to adventure and discover?

Which choice would be the *loving* one to make?

The father is wise enough to realize that if he always protected his son, the boy would never be able to become a man. Now it is very clear that the father has the power to keep his son completely *dependent* upon him, never open to danger or harm. But, for the sake of his son and a possible meaningful life for him, the father withholds some of his power that his son may have a future.

But now, suppose that means that, when he is learning to climb the stairs to the second floor, the boy stumbles and falls all the way down. Can a loving father permit that to happen? Yes, if the lad is to learn to climb stairs, even that risk must be permitted. But, suppose, when the boy grows older, he should choose to accept the values of friends who are not good for him. After giving his son every good direction and guidance, should a loving father permit his son to choose something the father would not like? Yes, part of love means that a father would permit his child to make his own choices, even ones the father does not approve. We might want to ask, "How could a loving father permit such a thing to happen to his own son?" But as we think about the alternative, should the son *not* have that freedom, we realize that love could no nothing else! But now a harder question. Suppose the father agrees not always to control and protect his son — because that is what a loving father must do. But suppose after freeing his son to go out adventuring into the world, somebody who does not like the father or the son approaches the boy by surprise one day and kills him! How wrong and unfair and undeserving to both the father and the son. Should we ask the question again? "How could the father permit that to happen to his son, when he had the power to keep the boy at home. What kind of father *is* that?"

It seems to me that the answer is clear: he is a *loving* father. And when he limited his power for his son's good, he also took a terrible risk which every parent must take. And his son's death would make the father grieve deeply. But he is very much a loving and caring father.

In many ways our Father in Heaven can be described by such an illustration. We *do* believe in a God of love. But he is also a God who has taken a terrible risk by allowing freedom in his creation. Some of the results of freedom are love and obedience and that which is good. But it also means tht there will be evil, and disobedience, and tragedy. It will mean that some things will happen that are unfair and cruel. Even people who love and serve God will be hurt and will suffer. Cannot God in his power destroy such unhappy and unfair things? Of course he can. But it is the choice faced by a father in a human family. Shall he protect his child from all harm? Or shall he risk even tragedy for his child's sake?

There is much that happens that is not God's will. But he is a loving God who suffers *with* his children when *they* suffer. That is the meaning of Jesus' terrible death on the cross. God was showing that he suffers with his children when they suffer.

We have God's promise — *not* that we will escape the trials, and even the terrors, of this world — but rather his promise that he is faithfully near and with his people in all things. St. Paul says in Romans 14 that "whether we live or die, we are the Lord's." Those are words of promise. They mean that nothing can separate us from God's love. Not even death itself.

Thank God that that is true!

NO EASY WORDS OF COMFORT
David A. MacLennan

*Preached at the funeral of a six-year-old girl who was **struck by a car.***

†††

Jesus said, "See that you do not despise one of these little ones; for I tell you that in heaven their angels always behold the face of my Father who is in heaven. (Matthew 18:10, RSV)

When a little child dies, no easy words comfort us. Even to the strong Christian believer, the death of a child seems so senseless, so wasteful, so inconsistent with all we know of our heavenly Father. Jesus loved and welcomed little children. He made them the type of person who is fit for the Kingdom of Heaven. "Truly, I say to you, unless you turn and become like children, you will never enter the kingdom of heaven," he said. (Matthew 18:3) Yet today we are met to worship God who is love and to pay our tribute of love to a child suddenly take from the family where she was so much loved. Before life's day had scarcely begun for Martha, it seems to have ended cruelly. What can we say to lessen our grief of hearts sorely hurt by this sorrow? Rather, what can the Lord himself say to them and to us to lighten the burden of bereavement, and to brighten the darkness in our souls?

First, Jesus our Lord speaks the same words of assurance he spoke during his earthly life. "And calling to him a little child, he put him in the midst of them, and said, 'Truly, I say to you, unless you turn and become like little children, you will never enter the kingdom of heaven. Whoever humbles himself like this child, he is the greatest in the kingdom of heaven!" To be like children is to have many lovely characteristics — the capacity to wonder, to forgive easily, to forgive the pain and heartache, to love freely those who are loving, to play. You may be sure that this dear girl is at home in what a poet called "the nurseries of heaven."

To be as a child is to be dependent. Just as she depended on her parents so, in the unseen home God prepares for all who love him, she will depend on the love and care of the One who loves little children and loves them forever.

Again, we should be comforted by Christ's beautiful affirmation: "for I tell you that in heaven their angels always behold the face of my Father who is in heaven." The New English Bible translators give the translation "their guardian angels." (Matthew 8:10) Jesus had issued a stern warning to any one who "causes one of these little ones who believe in me to sin." He also spoke encouragingly to those who welcomed a child and who love him and her and help the child to know God. This, said our Savior, is to welcome and help Christ himself. The best teacher and helper of a child is the Christian mother in the home, or the one who has taken the mother's place. Even though Martha has left her mother for a time, the mother's reward is great.

More than most people today, the ancients believed that every child had its guardian angel. To say that the angels always beheld the face of God meant that they had direct contact with God. Jesus is saying that, in God's sight, children are so precious that their guardian angels have the right of immediate access to the heavenly throne at all times. If this is so, we may confidently believe that the little one whose earthly life has ended is in the keeping of "Love Divine, all loves excelling." Even now, God is doing all that perfect love can do for the one so greatly loved.

In Matthew 18:44, there is the wonderful assurance that "it is not the will of my Father who is heaven that one of these little ones should perish." Just as a normal human parent would never permit a child to be lost, so will our heavenly Father guard and guide the life now continuing beyond our sight. Our blessed Lord has not told us any details of heaven, but he did tell us that he will be there, and where he is, all will be well. All *is* well with dear Martha now in his near presence. The child of so much love, for whom so many prayers have been offered, who is of supreme value to our Lord and heavenly Father, is safe and safe forever. She may not come to us but we may go to her. Be not anxious about your dear child, John and Helen, says the Lord of life and conqueror of death. Her angel is always in touch with God. Your heavenly Father will never let her go, or stumble, or be hurt. And God himself shall wipe away all tears from her eyes.

IT IS WELL
R. Blaine Detrick

Preached at the funeral of an eleven-year-old boy whose death by drowning in a nearby lake disrupted not only his family, but the parish family and the community as well.

✝✝✝

At a time of grief and sorrow and heartache, the Holy Spirit is our Comforter, speaking peace to our souls, providing heavenly strength, granting divine power, reassuring our hearts, deepening our faith, and increasing our hope.

Here again the words of Jesus himself:

"I will pray the Father, and he shall give you another Comforter, that he may abide with you forever."

"The Comforter, who is the Holy Spirit, whom the Father will send in my name, he shall teach you all things."

"Peace I leave with you, my peace I give unto you; not as the world giveth, give I unto you. Let not your heart be troubled, neither let it be afraid."

"In the world ye shall have tribulation; but be of good cheer; I have overcome the world." (John 14:16, 26, 27; 16:33)

Or listen to the words of a great hymn:

"When peace like a river attendeth my way,
When sorrow like sea billows roll,
Whatever my lot, Thou hast taught me to say,
'It is well, it is well with my soul.' "

At a time like this, when we find ourselves in the presence of unexplainable circumstances, of sudden and tragic events, in the awesome and mysterious presence of death, the mind says to the heart that it is easy for someone who has not suffered to speak such words, that it is easy for a hymn-writer to praise God in a time of happiness, blessing, and joy.

Let me remind you of a true incident. Mrs. H. G. Spafford, the wife of a Christian lawyer, was on her way to Europe, with their four children, aboard the French streamer, the *Ville du Havre.*

Early in the morning of November 22, 1873, the streamer was rammed by the English sailing vessel, the *Lochearn.* Damage was so severe that the *Ville du Havre* sank in twelve minutes. Although the mother was miraculously saved, she was in deep despair, for all of four of her daughters had been lost in the sea.

One can only begin to imagine the physical suffering and the mental anguish through which this beautiful lady passed. In her deep distress, however, she lifted up her soul unto God and renewed her faith, repeating to herself these words, "I won't be a fairweather friend to God. I will trust him, and someday I'll understand."

When her husband back home finally received the tragic word, he, too, endured a terrific struggle of the soul. Just a short time previously, he had lost almost everything in the terrible Chicago fire of October 8, 1871. Now, his family was decimated. This was a calamity beyond belief. In agony, Mr. Spafford walked the floor all night after he received the dreadful news. At length, he turned to a friend, who had been waiting with him, and quietly said, "I am glad to trust the Lord when it will cost me something."

As quickly as possible, he made plans to join his wife in Europe. One afternoon the captain called the lawyer into his cabin and told him that, according to his calculations, they were passing the place where the *Ville du Havre* had been wrecked.

After a period of quiet and thoughtful meditation, his faith came through strong and triumphant. There, on the high seas, near the place where his children had perished, he wrote,

"When peace like a river attendeth my way,
When sorrows like sea-billows roll,
Whatever my lot, Thou hast taught me to say,
'It is well, it is well with my soul.' "

These words did not come out of calm peace and prosperity, but were born out of severe struggle and heavy grief.

Jesus, our Lord, we need to remember, was a "man of sorrows and acquainted with grief." He knew, first-hand, the meaning of anguish, what it meant to be "despised and rejected of men." (Isaiah 53:3) Yet it was he who "endured the cross, despising the shame" (Hebrews 12:2) and who says unto us:

"Come unto me, all ye that labor and are heavy-laden, and I will give you rest."

"I will send the Comforter unto you."

"Peace I leave with you, my peace I give unto you."

"In the world ye shall have tribulation; but be of good cheer; I have overcome the world." (Matthew 11:28; John 16:7; 14:27; 16:33)

This story is told vividly and completely by a daughter of the H. G. Spaffords, born after the tragedy, in the book *Our Jerusalem*, by Bertha Spafford Vester, Doubleday and Company, Inc., Garden City, New York, 1950, chapters 3 and 4.

SWALLOWED UP IN VICTORY
Charles L. Koester

*Preached at the funeral of a seventeen-year-old young man who had just
graduated from high school. He was walking over to say goodbye to his
girlfriend, because he was to leave for the Navy the next morning, and
was stricken by a drunk driver.*

†††

Death is swallowed up in victory. For where now O death is
your power to hurt us? Where now O grave is the victory you
hoped to coin? All thanks be to God who gives us the victory
through our Lord Jesus Christ.

In these terrible moments of tragedy that engulf a family, relatives,
neighbors, and friends, several questions loom large before us. We have
each asked them of ourselves. We have asked them together. Why Mike?
Why so young? Why this way?

The answers to those ultimate questions we do not possess, nor can
any fellow human being give them to us. From our human reason, we
attempt to reach logical and rational conclusions, but to this tragedy of
life's termination, logic and reason do not apply. We know this. We know
this with a certainty. Yet, we still insist, in our own individual and
several ways, on being logical.

We will not so find an answer to those questions we ask from our
depths. Yet, we cannot dismiss our questioning, try as we will. Our
questions are human, and we are human.

We will question, too, the justice meted out to a drunk driver. In
frustration, we may quote the Old Testament which says, "an eye for an
eye, a tooth for a tooth." In anger, we will forget that Jesus Christ added
to that Scripture, "but I say unto you, you shall love your neighbor as
yourself."

Questions, questions, all kinds of questions. Our grief in this tragedy
is deep from inside us where we really live. Our feelings and emotions
are part of our humanness.

You each sit here, as I stand here, with your own set of questions.
Questions for which none of us will find the answers.

However, we have an alternative to our questioning, our grief, our
feelings of injustice and anger. It is God's alternative, and I would bring
it to each of us here this afternoon.

We can live life now, and from this day forward, in a futile, endless,
bitter grief — a grief which questions, but will find no answers. St. Paul
put it pointedly, as he said, "Truly, if our hope in Christ were limited to
this life only, we should, of all men, be most miserable." The other
alternative; we can live life now, and from this day forward, in a
redeeming grief. A grief that will again see the light of day, as it sees, as
well, the light of eternal life.

Even in sorrow we do have hope, and eternal hope is so clearly ours in Jesus Christ. That is what Christmas, Good Friday, and Easter are all about. He was born, he lived, he died, he rose, alive again! His empty tomb proclaimed that we are not empty. His ever living presence within us can fill us with the very presence of God.

Mike is with God, through Christ, the one whom he claimed as his Savior. He has more life today than any of us here. The certainty of our faith tells us this, strengthens us, comforts us, and, yes, redeems our grief.

"He who believes in me shall never die, but shall have everlasting life," said Christ. This assurance of our Lord is the beginning of our redeeming grief. We know where Mike is, and who he is with. Christ assures us, "He is with me. He is with me in my Father's house." With this assurance, our grief is redeemed, and we can continue to face life in this world with steady eyes. For even in this tragedy, there is the strength, the assurance, of life's destiny.

Don, Gerry, Diane, Jody, in your grief and loss, behind it all, underneath it all, in those empty places where you really live, Christ is present and ready to fill you with himself and with the presence of God. In loneliness, heartache, frustration, he says, "Cast your burdens upon me, for I care for you." God's Christ can redeem your grief, and give you God's peace that passes even our human understanding of it.

Death, even Mike's death, is swallowed up in victory through Christ. Mike lives! What a great comfort and strength it is to lean on the strong assurance of our Lord who said, "Because I live, you shall live also."

Life without such certain assurance of destiny would be a cruel joke played by a capricious God. A God whom all of us would reject. But God does not laugh from his Heaven at the hell of our heartache. He does not turn away from us, as we are so prone to turn away from him. Nor is he silent during the long night of our anguish of soul at the time of tragedy in the loss of a son, a brother, a friend. Nor does he leave us as empty, hollow shells of misery in our grief. No. God will have none of that!

Listen to the words of the Psalmist:
"The Lord will give strength unto his people.
The Lord will bless his people with peace."

You are the people of God. His people. And he will fill you with his peace and presence. Thanks be to God for the victory, even over death, through Jesus Christ our Lord.

Don, Gerry, Diane, and Jody, let us comfort one another with the hope, strength, and assurance of God's Word. Allow God's sent Son to redeem your grief. Mike is in God's good hands, in God's good House. Because Christ's victory is eternal, our separation from a loved one is not eternal, but temporary. Let us comfort one another with the victory Christ has accomplished for our lives, and for our faith.

Mike has abundant life eternal. And even in our tears, we would say, "Thank you, God. Thank you very, very much."

AN ACCIDENT OR A KNOCK AT THE DOOR
Leif Monson

Preached at the funeral of a young man, age twenty, who was thrown from an overturned car. Desperate efforts of the medical profession to save his life were futile.

†††

Behold, I stand at the door and knock; if any one hears my voice and opens the door, I will come in to him and eat with him and he with me. (Revelation 3:20)

Had newspapers been invented then, the following might have appeared in the Jerusalem *Times-Herald* on the Saturday after Good Friday: "Jesus of Nazareth, the son of Joseph and Mary was suddenly taken from his place of prayer in the Garden of Gethsemane, tried on charges of treason and blasphemy and hanged on a cross. The presiding judge, the honorable Pontius Pilate, made a last ditch effort to stay the judgment of death, but the unreasonable will of the mob would not be denied and he was crucified. Only thirty-three years old when he died, but rumored that he would rise again from the death. We know nothing of this for it has never happened before."

So far the story, but it didn't end there, for after his Resurrection did take place, his death has been used of God as his calling card to the world, for, "Behold, I stand at the door and knock; if any one hears my voice and opens the door, I will come in to him and eat with him and he with me."

In like manner, the following story could appear in the next edition of the *Walnut Grove Tribune:* "Gale Leiferman, son of Bernard and Algene Lieferman was suddenly thrown from his overturned car on a lonely stretch of road south of Walnut Grove. His lady companion summoned help and he was rushed to the hospital in Tracy and from there to Minneapolis. The doctors made a last ditch effort to stay the hand of death, but they were denied success. Only twenty years old at the time of his death, rumor has it he would rise again, but there are few who know of this for it has never happened before."

Again, so far the story, but it doesn't end here, for this accident became a calling card, a calling card of the Risen Son for he came into the world to stand at the door and knock.

Jesus of Nazareth came from God. Gale came from man. This ancient Jew could and did rise from the dead while Gale for the time being could not. This Man from Galilee came as Redeemer while Gale came to be redeemed. Yet, for all these differences and opposites, we find them one in death and the Risen Savior has entrusted to us to give meaning and purpose to that death.

Without the death of Christ, Gale's death would be meaningless, but without Gale's death, the death of Christ becomes some dusty and ancient event without meaning or relevance today. We cannot say that one died long ago and the other died last week for, in the council of heaven, when one dies the other dies, and if one lives the other shall live also. Neither can say that one was God and the other only a man, because even God became man. Nor can we say that one was old and the other young because both were young in years. Life was ahead of them, but instead of living to a ripe old age, they became calling cards to be used of God to call you and me unto himself.

In a strange and wonderful way, the Risen Christ calls Gale and Gale's death calls you — calls you to look — calls you to live and calls you to love. For if God gave us his Son to death on a cross that the world might be saved, this young man has been given up that you might be called. By the miracle of Christ, an accident has been changed to a knock at the door.

You may never have experienced the death of Jesus Christ. Maybe some of you will experience the death of Gale Leiferman, for his accident has become a knock at the door and a call to look, love, and live.

You came her to look — you answered the call of this boy's death, but what else have you seen? Have you gone back through history to see him, crowned with thorns, blood flowing from his hands and feet? Have you seen the whiplash crawl up and down his back or the crowds snapping out like human pyrannas, eager to get to this place of violence which preceded and caused the death of God? We claim to love peace and yet we become the daily victims of the violence which we create.

You came here to look, but what else have you seen? From his view on the cross, the Son of God sees a world gone mad, but this is precisely the world he's come to redeem for "Behold, I stand at the door and knock; if anyone hears my voice and opens the door, I shall come in to him and sup with him and he with me." He came to bind up the brokenhearted, to give real peace to those in conflict and call unto himself those in the agony of distress.

You came here to see because you were called, but there is more to see than a young man. There is more than the heaviness of despair. There is also light emerging from the darkness for, while Gale is dead, Jesus Christ has risen from the dead and his cry roars across the centuries, "Look at yourself! Look at your world! Then look at me!"

It is for you that he knocks and, while this knock began as an accident in a ditch, it doesn't end until it reaches the very gates of heaven with those who have heard, for he stands at the door and knocks.

If by this death you are called to look, you are also called to LIVE.

Fortunately, we don't remember the day of our birth, but doctors tell us that birth is accompanied by pain, suffering, and change by the one being born. If the child had known what awaited him during the process of birth, he might never have chosen to be born, content instead to rest in the security of his mother's womb. In their case at least, a call to live in this world has its beginning with the pains of birth.

And the call to live in his Kingdom is no different. It is accompanied by the pains of a new birth.

Standing outside the tomb of Lazarus, Jesus called him to live and he rose from the dead. Leaning over the bed of a little girl, he took her dead hand in his and she arose. Standing next to his tomb, God called to his Son and told him to rise again and he rose on the third day after his death, but the time is now here when the Risen Son is calling you to live and those who hear shall live. He calls you through the death of this one man.

Death is not a call to oblivion or meaninglessness. It's a call to live and those who fear death — those who hate it, curse it, or wish it would never come — are only rejecting the life which follows. Because there can be no life without death, God in his mercy allows death to happen so that through the death of one, many may be called to live.

If birth is God's call to a child to come into this world, death finds the same God calling us to come into his kindgom.

But if through their death we are called to look and live, through the same death we are called to LOVE.

During times of great stress, pain, and suffering, many only learn to hate. Some learn to hate God whom they presume to be the cause of all this grief. Others learn to hate the world which brings such afflictions upon us. Some might hate the doctors because they were unable to save life. In grief, some lash out at anything or anyone who happens to be nearby, thus increasing the pain and making the burden heavier to bear.

In contrast to this is the call to love by the things we have suffered. Suffering is no guarantee of love, but love seldom comes except by suffering.

There is the call to love DEATH.

It was his love of death that caused Paul to confess, "I would rather be away from the body and at home with the Lord," and it was the same love of death that led him to proclaim that the sufferings of this present world are not to be compared to the glory to be revealed to those who are called by his Name.

If a growing love of death seems morbid and cheerless for some, then let it be so, but this love of death grows because of the life beyond it and it is one of the great loves growing Christians have in common with each other.

Jesus also had a love of death in mind when he told the disciples, "Love your enemies," for man's greatest enemy is death, but for those who live in Christ and abide in him, death becomes an open door rather than a closed prison. A working servant to be loved rather than a cruel and meaningless master to be hated and feared.

There is also a call to love the WORLD.

The very familiar John 3:16, "For God so loved the world that he gave his only Son" could be made to read, "God gave his only Son so that he might love the world," for when Christ died on the cross, he called on his Father to love the world and seek it's redemption. Showing the Father his broken body, the crucified Nazarene says, "Look what the world has done to me." Then pointing to the Resurrection three days later, the same Savior could say, "Look what we can do for the world." Because of his death, God can love the world and raise it from the dead.

But this call to love the world is not far from any one of us. Who, but one who suffers, can understand and perhaps love another who has suffered? Who can comfort the afflicted but those who have passed through the afflictions themselves? We can understand the sickness of another if we have had the same sickness — God can understand the loss of a Son because he, too, lost his Son, but his loss is not wasted on self-pity, for by it he gains a greater and more compassionate love for you, and by the loss of your son, you may gain a greater and more compassionate love for the world.

There is the call to love ONE ANOTHER.

If you learn to love the world by the things you have suffered, you learn to love one another in the same way for it seems that death can bring about a closer family and community unity than any other event. This has always been the purpose of the death of the Son of God, for by his death we learn to love each other and we learn it again and again by the death of family members.

Finally, there is also a call to love LIFE, the necessary "other side" to the love of death.

At the same time, this call to love life is also a call to reject those things which try to pass muster as life. For those who won't love death can't love life either. They only love that which poses as real living.

Some think life is a big joke while the concern of others is only what they will eat, drink, and wear. Some in this community assume that life is a big martini in one hand and a six pack in the other, while still others think it to be nothing more than being busy or getting carried away by noise and lights, the use of drugs or the mighty plan we make for human success and the overabundance of the world's goods.

For the moment at least, this is all gone, but life isn't gone. The trappings, the past, the tinsel, and the falsities of life have been stripped away and real life remains to be discovered, and the death of this boy and of Jesus Christ is your call to enter into that life and make those discoveries.

With the death of the young, many begin to ask meaningful questions about life and death — questions seldom asked when the aged or the infirm are taken from us. The lesser things are swept away by the tidal wave of death. They become trash and human beings, perhaps for the first time, are thrust into the necessity of questioning everything they've ever believed about life and death.

No — Gale's death is not in vain, except for those who turn a deaf ear to the call that he brings, a call to look, to live, and to love. Gale's death is not just an accident, but a knock, for "Behold I stand at the door and knock. If anyone hear my voice and open unto me, I shall come in to him and sup with him and he with me" and in the process he shall be given vision, life, and love.

Funeral Sermons for Other Circumstances

THE BATTLE FOUGHT: THE VICTORY WON
O. Garfield Beckstrand II

Preached at the funeral of a woman who was widowed before the Great Depression, and whose life was a continual struggle. At age eighty, her body simply wore out.

†††

In the spirit of Christian hope and joy we gather this afternoon to give thanks to Almighty God for the life of our departed mother and grandmother, loved one and friend, Emilie Hall. How appropriate it is that we who have known and loved Mrs. Hall through the years gather in this sanctuary to pay tribute not only to her life and work, but also to her faith in God as she knew him through Jesus Christ.

I have been at a loss to find a fitting text for our meditation. How can one verse capture the essence of a life which has been so heroically, courageously, so faithfully lived, a faith which has been so humbly served, so nobly witnessed, and so unselfishly given as Mrs. Hall's? Only a cluster of verses could express our thoughts and feelings.

Knowing her simple faith in God we could say, "Blessed are the dead which die in the Lord from henceforth, yea, saith the spirit, that they may rest from their labors."

Knowing the quality of her life we could say in the words of the Psalmist, "Precious in the sight of the Lord is the death of his saints."

Knowing the faithfulness which characterized everything she did, we could say in the words of Jesus, "Well done, good and faithful servant, enter thou into the joy of thy Lord."

Knowing her dedication and devotion for her Lord, his church, and her family, we could say with St. Paul, "I have fought the good fight, I have finished the course, I have kept the faith; henceforth, there is laid up for me a crown of righteousness."

Knowing her childlike trust in God, her prayer would be the prayer of our Lord: "Father, into Thy hands I commend my spirit."

And for those of us who have known, loved, and respected Mrs. Hall through the years, we could say with the writer of Proverbs, "The memory of the just is blessed."

If Mrs. Hall were to express herself, she would say, "Garfield, don't speak about Emilie Hall; speak about my Savior." Let us ponder for a few moments some of the blessings which this hour brings to us.

Mrs. Hall was a woman of great faith. Her faith in God was not something which came from the writings of men, nor was it something which came to her on an intellectual plane. She did not need logical proof for the existence of God, for God was real to her. He was ever-present. He knew her and her needs. Her faith was strengthened, refined, and polished on the anvil of everyday experiences.

As a widow at age thirty-nine, she forged a beautiful life of service and raised two fine children, despite overwhelming obstacles. The needs of the day, whether it was strength for the burden, food for the table, or courage for the task, were met as she talked with her heavenly Father and depended daily upon him for his gifts.

Her faith was not a way of life which she claimed only for herself; it was a spirit which she shared with others. Her talents were always at the disposal of her Lord and his church. Her answer to service was always one word: "Yes." For over thirty years she played the piano for the Sunday School worship services. She conducted a church orchestra for a number of years. She was always available to teach and give expression to that faith which guided her life. Faithfully, year after year, she played for the Wednesday evening prayer meetings. Whether in sickness or health, in sorrow or joy, in exhaustion or leisure, she gave her talents freely to these services.

Every Wednesday morning last fall, winter, and spring she attended my Bible class. At eighty years she was eager to learn and to gain more insight into the Bible which she knew so well and loved so well.

Her faith meant worshiping God. As vital as food to the body, worship was nourishment for her soul on Sunday morning. Easter Sunday, 1909, as a girl of twenty-two, she joined Trinity Church. Rarely since that Sunday has she missed a service of worship or the Sacrament of Holy Communion.

People today may deny the existence of God. They may claim that he does not know individuals and that he does not care for them personally. But the life of our departed speaks with clarity beyond all logic, with assurance above all proof, and with confidence over all doubt that God lives and loves and cares for his children.

Mrs. Hall knew the meaning of life and death. She knew that life's purpose here upon earth was to serve God and his children. So beautifully she labored many times in the early morning hours or in the late evening hours to make a cake, to write a greeting or poem, or to perform some other task to bring joy and goodwill, love, and understanding to her loved ones and friends. Life, for her, was not to receive, but to give, that the light of God would shine through the troubles and problems of the day.

She knew also the meaning of death. She knew that the hour would come when the day's tasks would be done and the opportunities to serve would be over. She could say with the hymn writer:

Some day the silver cord will break
And I no more as now shall sing;
But, O, the joy when I shall wake
Within the palace of the King!
And I shall see him face to face
And tell the story — saved by grace!

We rejoice in that promise that to be separated from earth means to be joined in Heaven. Heaven is not only a place of separation from earth; it is a place of eternal security, peace, and joy. Locked out is sickness, sorrow, pain, and death. Locked out forever are heartaches, frustrations, disappointments, and doubt. Secure indeed are the treasures of God. Jesus said: "I go to prepare a place for you, that where I am, there you will be also." Whatever heaven has in store, we rest with the assurance that in the eyes of God death is gain, life's finest gift, and life's greatest reward. In that triumphant faith we can say with the poet:

Servant of God, well done!
Rest from thy love employ:
The battle fought, the victory won,
Enter thy Master's joy.

The pains of death are past;
Labor and sorrow cease,
And life's long warfare closed at last;
Thy soul is found in peace.

GOD'S PROMISES, PROMISES!
John R. Brokhoff

In my Father's house are many mansions; if it were not so, I
would have told you. I go to prepare a place for you. And if I go
and prepare a place for you, I will come again, and receive you
unto myself; that where I am, there ye may be also. (John 14:2, 3)

A former student of mine tells this boyhood experience about his
father's promises. When he was an eight-year-old lad, his father
promised him a BB gun for which he longed with intense desire. His dad
promised that when his next paycheck came, they would get the gun. In
those days, work was scarce and his father only had a part-time state
job. On the day when the check was due to arrive, it rained and the road
was muddy. The check came on time, but with it was a letter ordering
him to come to Atlanta, two hundred miles away, that very day. The boy
knew that his father could not drive in the rain to town twenty miles
away, come back with a gun, and then drive to Atlanta. To keep his
father from seeing his disappointment, he slipped up to his room and
sobbed with a broken heart. He heard his mother and dad whispering to
each other while his mother packed a bag for his father. Then he heard
the front door slam and the leaving of the car. He wept himself almost to
sleep, but sometime later he was awakened by a familiar sound of a horn.
It was his dad. He rushed to the front porch and saw his Dad holding out
a BB gun to him. He ran down and took it. Neither he nor his father had a
word to say. There was no need of saying anything. His dad drove off to
Atlanta. Years later the student, now a prominent minister, said that
when anyone said anything about the promises of the Heavenly Father,
he had no difficulty believing them because he had this experience with
his earthly father's promises. If an earthly father could keep his
promises, how much more would the Heavenly Father keep his
promises!

On this occasion, when our hearts are broken because of the loss of a
loved one, we hear some promises of the Father through his Son, Jesus
Christ. These promises, if accepted and trusted, will bring us comfort
and peace in our sadness.

In our text Jesus promises us that there is room in heaven for all of
God's people. He said, "In my Father's house there are many mansions
... " In other words, there is room for everyone who dies in Christ. It is
not true that heaven has a limited enrollment. We cannot say that only
144,000 are allowed to be in heaven. Heaven is big enough for all those
who put their trust in God.

Isn't this good news for us who sorrow over the passing of a loved
one? We need not worry whether there was room for him. All of us know
that when we take a trip to an important and popular place (Heaven is as
popular a place as one can find, for who does not want to go to Heaven?)
that there is always a question whether or not we will be able to get
reservations. Usually we seek reservations weeks in advance to be sure

there will be a place or room for us. The marvelous thing about this promise is that we need not make reservations with God to get living space in heaven. There is room for all who die in Christ. No one will be left out. God will not treat any of his children like men once treated his Son when there was no room in the inn for Jesus to be born.

In our text, Jesus makes another promise to us. He tells us that he is going ahead of us to prepare a place for us in heaven. Hear his words: "I go to prepare a place for you."

In human relations we know that when we expect visitors or guests in our homes, we make preparations for them. We stock up on food and drink that there will be plenty on hand when the guests arrive. The housewife gives the house a good cleaning. Special meals are prepared. Before guests arrive, the house is in a hubbub of preparation. If this is the case with human guests in our homes, would it also not be true that God through Jesus makes preparations for his children to come to their eternal home? What kind of preparation does Jesus make for us to come to heaven? It is a spiritual preparation.

This preparation is necessary because the Bible tells us that when every one of us dies, we must appear before God, the righteous judge. God is infinite and holy. We are finite and sinful. We cannot stand before Almighty God in our own right, dressed in the filthy rags of our unworthiness and sins. Jesus has gone ahead to make things right with God. He made these preparations when he was on earth by dying on the cross for our sins and rising from the dead that we too might rise from death. On earth he fulfilled all the laws of God and completed all of God's demands of perfection. Now Jesus goes to God in heaven and says that in behalf of all men he has died for their sins and completed for man all that God asked of man. He begs God to forgive men on the basis of his own work and merits. That is why we say Jesus is our Mediator. He intercedes for us before God and he makes it possible for us to stand before God with the robe of righteousness given to us by Christ. When we die and appear before God, everything has been taken care of that we might be admitted to God's presence and accepted in love for Jesus' sake.

Is this truly not a comfort to each of us sinners? Now we need not worry about our loved ones or ourselves whom we confess to be sinners. For who is perfect? Jesus promised that he would go ahead and prepare a place for us in God's kingdom. To trust this promise will bring us comfort and encouragement.

In the words of Jesus, our text tells us of a third promise of the Father through Jesus. It is the promise that Jesus will be with us. That we will not be alone in heaven. Listen to the promise, "Where I am, there ye may be also."

We do not know who is going to be in heaven, except One. This one is Jesus himself. Indeed, there will be others, but no one can be certain that our friends and members of the family will be there. That is in God's hands. We can be sure that Jesus is there and that really is enough.

Have you ever wondered what heaven is like? Is it a place of pearly gates and streets of gold? Does anyone know about the "furniture" of heaven? No one can say what heaven is like. All we can do is paint pictures involving symbolism. But one thing we can be sure of: Christ promises that he will be there to greet and meet us when we arrive and ever stay with us. That is what makes Heaven. It is not necessarily a physical place with all kinds of jewels. It is a spiritual condition made possible by the presence of Jesus. Where he is, there is life and love and peace. Then to be in Heaven means to be in life, to be in love, to be at peace in Christ. Since this is so, why then should we lament the passing of a loved one who died in Christ? This dear one is far better off than we are on earth. He is experiencing the time of his life. He is saying, "This is real living!" Heaven is a glorious place where love, life, and joy abound.

You know, a promise is only as good as the one who makes it. Who made these promises about our going to heaven? It was none other than God speaking through Jesus to his disciples. Is there anyone greater or more trustworthy than God? Even if a great and reliable person makes a promise, we believe a promise until the time the person making the promise does not keep it. After that, we doubt whether any future promise will be kept. Can anyone ever claim that God at any one time or place ever broke a promise to man? Indeed, the truth is that God has always kept his Word. He will keep it now, and will always keep his Word. God is not capricious. God is steadfast, constant, and forever dependable. You can trust these promises of Christ. If you stand on these promises, you will have comfort and strength not only now in this hour of bereavement, but in all the days ahead.

WHEN LIFE FALLS IN ON US
Don R. Yocom

Preached at the funeral of a county sheriff who was an innovative law-man as well as an active church member and good Christian example in the community.

✝✝✝

Though he slay me, yet will I trust in him. (Job 13:15)

The hardest question we face in life is the question before us today. WHY? Life has in it many interrogation points: Where did I come from? Where do I go when I die? Why do the righteous suffer? Why do people die suddenly sometimes? WHY . . . WHY . . . WHY . . . For an answer I refer you to the oldest book in the Bible, the book of Job. When life falls in upon us, we can find some comfort and assurance from the famous words of the man from Uz, who said to his so-called friends, "Though God slay me, yet will I trust him." What a statement of faith that is!

We pick up our daily paper and read of the sudden death of someone and say, "Oh, my!" and then dismiss it from our thoughts because it does not concern our family or friends. But when it comes to us personally, or when it stuns an entire county, it becomes a different matter. We do not plan for the unexpected turn of events. Hopes and dreams are gone, and we hardly know where to turn. Life seems full of tragedies of one kind or another. When a man is doing a fine piece of work, something he enjoys, we glory in it with him. We are all saddened when he is cut down suddenly.

There are several ways we can react at a time like this. One way is to try to lay the blame on someone. Some try to blame God, others blame the man himself; but really, neither was to blame. Trying to lay blame so often leads to bitterness. But a reasonable person will not make God out as a murderer, though he permits things to happen. We torture ourselves and, worse than that, we torture the loved ones when we try to lay blame for such a death.

Another way to react is to try to escape the reality by withdrawing from everything. That doesn't solve any problems either.

Some people take a fatalistic point of view and say that this is the way it was supposed to be. Such a view is contrary to our Christian faith. As a pastor, I shall never be led to believe, in the light of God's Word, that God wills harm to anyone. Fatalism is but a shortcut idea of religion, and it shortcircuits vital faith. If God made us free to choose, he also is free to do or to permit as he sees fit. We do not know what might have happened if Bob Howard had lived. There are so many possibilities, such as being an invalid the rest of life or some other consequence, we finally conclude that there are worse things than to die suddenly.

One does not have to live to eighty years of age to have lived a full and significant life. If ever a man felt his responsibility and enjoyed it, it was Bob Howard. The day before he took the oath of office as Sheriff of Darke County he came to me and asked if I, as his pastor, would have prayer with him. We prayed together in my study, and afterward we talked about the office he was assuming. Margaret and I have observed how he enjoyed his work. He liked to talk about it before groups around the county. He met with the ministers of Darke County shortly after assuming office, and declared his intentions to do the very best he could as Sheriff. The attendance here at this service today is an indication of how well he has fulfilled his office. He didn't have to live to be an old man to have a worthwhile experience.

The real alternative for us is that we accept the reality of what has happened, and go on to live day by day a life of faith in a God who knows best. I'm sure that there are things that happen which God does not want. I cannot believe that he wants premature death, accidents, wars, and the unnatural pain from incurable illnesses. Yet, we also know that if God caused a miracle to happen every time one of us was stricken with illness or faced an accident, the laws of the universe would be eliminated one by one. No one has found a better way to run this universe, even if God does permit the accidental and sudden things to happen. God did not even spare his own Son, Jesus, when he died on a cross. It is written into the very nature of God's world. God suffers too! Therefore we know he cares. His Holy Spirit, the blessed comforter, assures us of his love and understanding.

Through the ages, Christians have learned that if we live for God by faith in Christ we have peace in our hearts. When we let God take over, we know the comfort and the power of his Holy Spirit is with us. We begin to get a mature understanding of how God works with us. If we can see that death is the door to eternal life, then, sudden as it may come, we have this hope that there is something greater and better for us ahead.

Another thought, in a very real sense, and not a superstitious one either, we can sense the immortal presence of those whose lives have meant so much to us. In our memories of the many good times we had with Bob Howard, in the various projects he started in his office and community, in activities of the home, also, we shall be reminded of him and know that though he cannot speak to us, his influence will live on. We shall remember him often, and know that he is not gone from us forever, but is just ahead of us on the way to God.

So we did not come here today to sorrow without hope. That hope springs eternal in the human breast. Mr. Howard would not want us to grieve for him. We must carry to completion the things he started, taking up the responsibilities he has laid down. Another person has taken his office and will deserve our prayerful support. And certainly we can look ahead with hope for eternity.

To those who come to pay respect to one whom we all knew and loved, I urge you to prepare ourselves for whatever the future has in store for you. How we face it determines our destiny, and it may influence the lives of many other people. Let us determine now that we shall be dedicated to this task. The consecration of Bob Howard should challenge us to be as consecrated to our task as he was to his.

DEATH AS A CELEBRATION
Heth H. Corl

Preached at the funeral for a church member who died of old age.

†††

Many of us have participated in the great celebrations of life: birth, baptism, confirmation, marriage. Each celebration gives reason for us to rejoice in God who has granted his blessing.

At this particular hour we have come to worship God in memory of (our loved one). Can we offer true worship to God if this service is not also considered a celebration? Of course, death is not a celebration if it destroys a person, or if it is the end of existence. But the Christian faith proclaims that death is a victory because of Christ. Listen to the doxology Paul quoted from the prophets in celebration of death:

Death is swallowed up in victory.
O death, where is thy victory?
O death, where is thy sting?
The sting of death is sin. . . . But thanks be to God, who gives
us the victory through our Lord Jesus Christ. (1 Corinthians
15:54b-57)

The memorial services for our loved ones in Christ are indeed celebrations! In these few moments we will consider what it is that death celebrates.

Death Celebrates a Victorious God

God is not defeated by death. Life and death are both in God's control. In life, God cares and provides for us. He gives us hope in the face of discouragement. He offers grace and love even when we do not deserve it. In death, God gives no less. Death represents man's complete inability to help himself. It causes us to see we are completely dependent on God. And when death seems so final, so powerful over man's weakness, God comes to make known his victory! The final enemy each of us must face is cast aside in defeat.

We are not saying that God keeps our bodies from dying a physical death. We are saying that death is ineffective in its power to destroy the person. Indeed, we believe that only then do we discover the real living that God has promised to us. Fears that haunt us; punishment we have deserved by sin; the seemingly end of an existence: All these are defeated by God who has conquered death. It is by God's victory that we share in a life that death cannot take from us. Death celebrates the victory of God in whom we have put our trust!

But there is more to this celebration:

Death Also Celebrates a Loving Savior

We know it is true, whether we have read it in the Bible or not, that "all have sinned and fall short of the glory of God." (Romans 3:23) We also know that "the wages of sin is death." (Romans 6:23a) Those facts are the source of man's greatest fears, his most severe anxieties. It is the story of man's life and man's death without the encouraging message of Christ. But because of him we have learned "the free gift of God is eternal life in Christ Jesus our Lord!" (Romans 6:23b)

Jesus did not come to condemn us. Our sins had already done that. Instead, Jesus came to share with us a salvation that begins here and now — a salvation not dependent on our righteousness, for even "while we were yet sinners, Christ died for us." (Romans 5:8) Christ shared with us a salvation that enables us to "come alive" — a coming alive that continues into eternity. The death of a Christian celebrates that salvation. Certainly this is reason to rejoice!

This joy increases as we grow into a new relationship with God. And so

Death Celebrates a Life Lived in Fellowship with God

Because of the salvation Christ shares with us, we are brought into a new relationship with God. The celebration of death is a witness of that companionship with God. God has created us in his image that we may be in fellowship with him. Because of sin, we deny his image and break that relationship. Then death is begrudged, even feared. But the salvation God has given through Christ restores his image in us and brings us back into fellowship with him. The Christian life then, is a new life lived in fellowship with God. The Christian's joy flows from that renewed fellowship like a cup running over. And so, in death, we celebrate a glorious life lived in companionship with God.

But death celebrates not only a companionship with God in this life. The real celebration of death is the fact that our fellowship with God will never end. Praise God for the fact that

Death Celebrates the Beginning of a Permanent Fellowship with God!

Jesus said, "I am the resurrection and the life; he who believes in me, though he die, yet shall he live, and whoever lives and believes in me shall never die." (John 11:25, 26) He proved that with his own resurrection. He also said, "Because I live, you shall live also." (John 14:19) And we all know many who have confidently faced death because of that assurance.

Even though we love God and want to serve him, we have difficulty in being what we want to be and what God wants us to be. In this life we never completely escape the grip of sin. We aim toward perfection, but our human nature prevents us from attaining it. But, by God's grace, he hears our penitent prayers. He forgives us, and accepts us into eternity where we are forever his. Then the limitations that sin imposes on us no longer have any power to threaten our relationship with God.

We are most truly ourselves when we are in a right relationship with God. Christians rejoice in death's celebration because it seals permanently our eternal existence in fellowship with God who created us to be his forever!

Our expression of worship today is a celebration. We are celebrating a victorious God who shares his victory with us. We are celebrating a loving Savior who has shared salvation with us. We are celebrating a life lived in fellowship with God. We are celebrating the reality of life that will be lived eternally with God. All this is reason to celebrate, to rejoice.

But where does that leave the hurt, the grief, the pain that we feel in our sorrow? Are we spiritually immature if we are saddened by our loved one's leaving us? No, we can celebrate and cry at the same time. Jesus wept at the grave, certainly not in denial of faith or of hope, but out of human pain that is a part of being a person. How many parents have rejoiced at their child's wedding, fighting back tears, not because they want their child back home, but because a new relationship is beginning quite unlike the old relationship? Hurt and happiness often times are a part of each other. But only for a little while. The pain of transition is soon healed by the comfort of God's Spirit as he continues to minister to his people, both those in this life as well as those in the life to come.

The victory is not that grief defeats joy, but rather that joy conquers grief. "Thanks be to God, who gives us this victory through our Lord Jesus Christ!" (1 Corinthians 15:57)

JESUS CALLED TO HER
T. A. Kantonen

Preached at the funeral of a forty-year-old woman who died a lingering death from cancer.

†††

And when Jesus saw her, he called to her and said to her, "Woman, you are freed from your infirmity." (Luke 13:12)

We have today a heartfelt sense of great loss. The family has lost a devoted wife and tender mother. The community has lost a leader whose competence and willingness could always be depended upon in every good enterprise. A vast circle of friends has lost a true and unselfish friend whose personality was radiant with understanding and sympathy. The church has lost not only a loyal member but also a talented and faithful worker who gave herself wholeheartedly to Christian service. Many of us are better because she was with us. We thank God for her and we bless her memory. God has spoken to us through her life and character. Today we wish to listen to what God speaks to us through her death.

The text of our meditation was selected many weeks ago when it became apparent that Helen would not recover, but that it was God's will to make her lingering illness the gateway into the life eternal. I had come to know her very well, and there is no other passage in the Word of God that I deem more fitting for this occasion.

Portrayed here is a scene from the latter days of our Lord's earthly ministry. He has entered a Galilean synagogue on a Sabbath day. As he looks over the congregation in the little church, his eyes become fixed upon one of the worshipers. It is a woman who has suffered for a long time. As the months and the years went by and the illness persisted, her body gradually lost its upright posture and she became bent as though she carried an invisible heavy burden. But she came to the Lord's house faithfully just the same, for her heart was there. Then came the day when her faithfulness was gloriously rewarded. She looks up and before her is the Savior himself. His lips move and he speaks, not to the congregation in general, but to her personally. It is a healing and redeeming word that he speaks, such as only the Savior can speak. "And when Jesus saw her, he called her and said to her, 'Woman, you are freed from your infirmity.' " While he speaks, his hand touches her and at once the binding shackles fall. She rises from her cramped posture, her body straight and strong, and she goes home praising God.

Against the background of this touching little story from the Bible, we think today of Helen. She, too, came faithfully to God's house and drew strength from his word. She, too, was given a heavy burden of suffering to bear through long weary days and nights which seemed never to end, a burden which strained every ounce of her endurance almost to the breaking point. Loving hands ministered to her, it is true, and everything within human reach was sought to alleviate the suffering. But the crushing burden was still there, to be borne day after day, week after week, month after month. Like her Master, as he writhed in the bitter agony of the cross, she, too, was forced to look up into the face of God and cry, "My God, why?"

To find the answer, she and her pastor were compelled to explore deeply the mysterious ways of God. Does not the Bible tell us that Christ himself was made perfect through suffering? He could not be the Savior that he is and enter so deeply into our sorrows, had he not been subjected to such pain and agony of his own. When the divine Craftsman holds us to the wheel of pain and the flames of suffering, when the chisel of agony stabs us, should we not press our lips together and not whimper, for is this not God's way of fashioning a more Christlike character? Does not the very fact of suffering show that there is something in us that is precious to God? Otherwise, he would not spend so much time and take so much care with us, as he puts us through the purifying and refining process. Can there be any genuine courage or sympathy or unselfishness without suffering? And when foundations are being dug very deep, is it not because a great and high structure is in the making?

These were some of the answers that God gave us. But the great lesson was to learn to trust God even when we could not understand his ways. More than once she found comfort in that faith of which the poet sang:

> Not till the loom is silent
> And the shuttles cease to fly,
> Shall God unroll the canvas
> And explain the reason why
> The dark threads are as needful
> In the weaver's skillful hand,
> As the threads of gold and silver
> In the pattern he has planned.

It was this faith that ripened into a quiet sustaining assurance as the sunset gradually passed and the shadows of night began to fall. Prayer became more and more fervent and Heaven more and more desirable. Faith lifted the clouds of pain and allowed God's love to shine through. Like the woman of our text, she looked to her Lord alone for the deliverance which no power on earth could bring. Resting upon the everlasting arms, she was concerned at the end not so much about herself as about others, anxious only about the worry and discomfort which her condition was causing to her loved ones.

At long last came the hour of deliverance. The Savior's eyes sought her out from our midst, his redeeming hand was placed upon her, and his lips spoke the liberating word, "Helen, you are freed from your infirmity, you have waited long enough, you are very tired, you have done your day's work, I will give you rest."

On my last pastoral visit, she could not longer open her eyes to see me or respond to my voice. A higher and better Pastor had taken charge. I could only commit her to his keeping with the beautiful words of the church's order for the commendation of the dying, "Depart in peace, thou ransomed soul."

To the bereaved, let me add this word of consolation. Helen's life and departure from this life preach a much better sermon than I could preach. We feel a sense of great loss, it is true, but we know that such a life is never lost. She has but entered another room in God's great house, where the Master of all good workmen has set her to work anew. She has been freed from infirmity to serve God in new strength and loveliness. And she continues to serve you, too, for her memory will inspire you to follow her and her Savior and to bind you closer to one another. Heaven will be all the more desirable to you because she has gone there before you. And so we do not sorrow as those who have no hope. We thank God for what he has given us through her and we pray:

> Lord Jesus, King of Paradise,
> O keep us in thy love,
> And guide us to that happy land
> Of perfect rest above;
> Where loyal hearts and true
> Stand ever in the light,
> All rapture through and through,
> In God's most holy sight.

THE SEASONS OF LIFE
Roger L. Tappert

Preached at the funeral of a man, age seventy, who was a farmer and auctioneer, well-known in his community, and a pillar of the church who had the wisdom to know how to be a pillar. He died after ten years of suffering from cancer.

✝✝✝

Text: Psalms 71

Today we affirm life! Our lives and the life of one whom we love. Psalm 71 is a song that affirms life. From youth to old age the Lord is our shelter for life and hope and love. Our hearts swell with a solemn joy — the joy of knowing that we have been created for life and that we have life forever in Jesus Christ.

Today we affirm life! Christ stands with us offering words of comfort — words that light our fear: "I am your life, I am your hope; you die no more, you live in me."

The life we affirm has seasons — like the year. Spring, summer, autumn, and winter. With God as our refuge, we live each season growing closer to him and understanding the order of his presence in our lives and in the universe.

1. We affirm spring. We affirm the bright, fresh days of our youth. Remember those days! The days of unlimited energy and health that wouldn't give up. We danced until two in the morning. We worked from sunup until sundown. I remember staying up all night to finish term papers for college; I can't do that anymore. Those were good days. We remember the spring of youth and we give thanks to God for those days and for his unfailing love toward us in those days.

2. We affirm summer. Gradually we grow up. We are moved from youth to maturity. We begin to stand back, to size up the situation, and to evaluate before we jump into a problem. We move with a more even pace. Our energy seems limited; our health seems to be softening. Cuts don't heal as quickly as they did when we were teenagers. World issues don't seem to be so pressing and solutions don't seem to be so clear. But we have wisdom — a gift that we have received from God, a gift that we have learned through the experiences of our youth. Trouble doesn't hurt. We know that our Creator is with us redeeming us out of all of our troubles. We enjoy our life. We are happy with life.

3. We affirm autumn. Spring and summer pass quickly. We grow older and autumn is with us. Life becomes beautiful. Preace is easier. God is with us and we know it. Christ presides at the feast of life and we know it. We bask in the love and hope and life of being God's children and we know it. I watch my friends fighting to gain a position in life — I look at myself and see the same fighting in my life. Then, I look at the older members of our community. They know life and affirm it. They know their Redeemer and they live at peace in him. I envy them. I look forward to autumn. I look forward to the days of peace and hope.

4. *We affirm winter.* And then, there is winter, the end of life. Usually, we experience sickness and then death. Sometimes we die quickly. Whatever the case, the inescapable fact of life is ours — we die. But winter is like autumn, a time of hope. We live in the day of resurrection. We affirm life — life in Jesus Christ. Jesus said, "If any man would come after me, let him take up his cross and follow me." (Matthew 16:24) We have followed. We have followed the seasons of life in the cross. We have been baptized into the body of Jesus Christ. We have died in him. We live in him. We die no more.

We affirm life from youth to death. We join the writer of Psalm 71 who says, "Lord, I put my hope in you; I have trusted in you since I was young. I have relied on you all my life; you have protected me since I was born; I will always praise you!"

We affirm life. We affirm the spring of our youth. We affirm the summer of living in wisdom. We affirm the autumn of living peacefully in the hope of Jesus Christ. We affirm the winter of old age — death. But, in affirming death, we affirm the new spring, the spring of life in Christ, eternal life which is beyond all seasons.

A MEMORIAL HYMN TEXT
("A SOLEMN JOY ENFOLDS OUR HEARTS")
Roger L. Tappert

A solemn joy enfolds our hearts,
    the Lord speaks words to light our fear;
"I am your life, I am your hope;
    you die no more, you live in me."

The spring of youth is bright and fresh
    enriched by God's unfailing love;
then summer casts an even pace
    and wisdom heals when trouble hurts.

The autumn of our days brings peace,
    we bask in love and hope and life;
then winter comes and brings us death,
    but freed by Christ, we live again.

A solemn joy enfolds our hearts,
    affirming life from youth to death;
O Jesus Christ we give you thanks,
    in life and death, you are our hope.

PAIN AND TRIUMPH
James A. Ray

Preached at the funeral of a man, age fifty-eight, who died of leukemia two years after his wife had died suddenly from a stroke. He was a faithful church member.

†††

Text: John 14:2-7

Death is a fact. A hard, painful, brutal fact. It strips a person of any facade, any mask he may have. As we stand in the face of death, it is a time for honesty, a time for truth. And the truth is that it hurts deep and long when someone we love dies.

One of the reasons for the pain we feel is because, over the years, a relationship of respect, trust, and love developes. When that relationship is ended by death, something of importance to us is gone. Our natural reaction is to rebel and say 'No,' this can't be! It must not be! It isn't right!"

Jesus knew it wasn't right, that it wasn't part of God's plan to have something good destroyed or ended with death. To change all that, Jesus allowed himself to be put to death, thus destroying all that is good and noble and perfect. But his death was only the beginning; he rose from death and restored all the relationships which had been broken when he died.

Never again could death destroy the relationship a Christian has with his Lord or the relationship Christians have with each other. Jesus' resurrection establishes a continuity from this side of the grave to the other. The living Christ is both here with us, and there, with those who, like Roy have died following him.

So the funeral of this Christian is two things: It is a time of profound sadness for those of us who knew him, loved him, and will miss him.

But this funeral is also a victory celebration. The victory has been won over death by Jesus' resurrection from the dead. That resurrection becomes the property of the followers of Christ. With Jesus' resurrection comes the victory over death for all who love him.

So, for the victory over death, for hope in the face of sadness, for all things, we thank and praise God through Jesus Christ.

EASTER IS NOW!
Arley Fadness

*Preached upon the death of a church member who had long suffered
from cancer.*

†††

May the eternal God whose power ranges over life and death comfort
and encourage you. May the Holy Spirit renew you in mind and heart.

We are gathered this afternoon because of the death of a dear and
beloved one. Emma ...... , ill for several months, passed away as a result
of a common and dreaded disease. Her suffering was intense. Her
struggle was valiant.

We have come to honor her memory and to give her God praise and
prayer in this worship service. It is good you are here. You are the ones
who were near and dear to her. You are the ones she called her friends,
her neighbors and, of course, her beloved family.

You, the family, have requested this verse from Revelation 2:10, to
serve as the basis of this sermon, "Be thou faithful unto death and I will
give you a crown of life."

This verse was spoken to the church at Smyrna in Asia Minor.
Smyrna was a sizable city located picturesquely on the Aegean Sea. A
Christian congregation had been established there. But soon in the first
and second centuries a terrible persecution took place. The emperors of
Rome — Nero, Domitian and others, pompously required of all their
subjects that *they* be worshiped as "Divine Lord." They commandeered
the confession of a false creed "Caesar is Lord" as a sign of political
allegiance. But the Christians at Smyrna refused to throw a pinch of
incense on the altar and profess that false and misleading creed. Rather,
they courageously proclamed, "Jesus is Lord."

And for that stand, for that confession of faith, they paid dearly in life
and limb.

And the saying got started, "The blood of the martyrs is the seed of
the church."

The aged John, whose revelation was a message to the church under
seige and bitter persecution, records the words of Jesus who is described
as holding the seven stars in his right hand. The words are: "I know your
tribulation, I know your poverty, I know your slander, do not fear, be
faithful unto death and I will give you a crown of life."

It is heartening to recall the struggles at Smyrna and the caliber of
her leadership.

Polycarp, early bishop of Smyrna may have known acquaintances of
Jesus. This courageous soul became a devoted disciple writing letters of
encouragement to congregations. Toward the end of his long and illus-
trious life he went to visit Anicetus, bishop of Rome to discuss the proper
date of Easter. While there, the Romans arrested him. Refusing to pay
homage to Caesar as Lord he was taken to the arena where opportunity
was given to deny Christ.

80

History has never forgotten Polycarp's reply, "Eighty and Six years have I served him and he never did me any injury. How then could I blaspheme my King and my Savior?"

Unable to bend his will, break his spirit or scare him, the Romans took Polycarp and burned him at the stake."*

Such was the faith of those members of the church at Smyrna.

The question of faithfulness can be a costly one. The question of faithfulness is always a personal one.

Faithfulness and Emma ...... were not strangers. She expressed to me her faith many times during her illness. Those of you who knew her and loved her knew what God in Jesus Christ meant to her.

Emma was a tall woman. I was talking with you members of the family about that. She was a tall mother with tall sons, but her tallness was not only in stature. She was tall in faith. She was tall in her loving service to others.

Rummaging through some books, I ran onto the meaning of the name Emma. In Old German, it means Universal One. In more modern German, it means Nurse. Nurse suggests to me one who serves others. One who binds up our wounds, who is an expert at comforting and caring.

Above all a Nurse must be faithful, as a mother is faithful, a true friend is faithful. So we thank God for Emma.

"Be faithful, be faithful." Like a recurring theme in a symphony, it hums its way through the book of revelation and through the Scriptures from beginning to end.

"Do not fear, be faithful and I (that is Jesus, the Resurrected One) will give you the crown of life. The Christians then and now never forget that — they live by that. "Be faithful" is the call to those of us who are yet alive by Christ who himself was faithful — obedient even to death on the cross.

They would continue to suffer persecution, they would endure tribulation those early Christians, some would be tempted to give up, quit — yet, the emerging theme of the Book of Revelation grasps us firmly and comfortingly, "Have courage for today and hope for tomorrow. God has the final word."

Maintaining this stance in a world at war with death is not easy.

The church meant a lot for Emma.

I'm so glad for the church. Faithful. Supporting. Hopeful. I'm glad to experience the rhythm of the liturgical lifebreath of the church. Lent is death. But Easter is Resurrection and victory and life.

Easter is now. Life. Heaven. Saints singing, "Worthy is the Lamb who was slain."

How could those Christians at Symrna face their own personal Lenten experiences of suffering and death without the faithfulness of God to sustain in the end?

May you be strengthened in the knowledge that Easter has the last word. The crown of life goes to him who is faithful.

---

*Candles in the City, G. Curtis Jones, Word Book Publishers, Waco, Texas. p. 25, 26.

Funeral Sermons for Unique Occasions

DO WE TRAVEL IN FEAR OR IN FAITH?
Edwin R. Lincoln

Preached at a Communion Service of Remembrance for five persons of a group within the church who, over the years, had died. This memorial service is conducted each year, remembering all deceased members.

Text: Hebrews 11:1-10, 13-16; 12:1-3

The writer of this letter has just asked us a question: "How are we gathered here today? With what mind do we approach this moment of memorial?" To be sure, there is the fact of love and remembrance which accounts for our presence here. The death of a friend diminishes each one of us. These persons we think about today enriched and completed our lives. But the writer of Hebrews is also asking us in what manner we travel through all the events of life, of which death is one. Do we travel in fear or in faith?

If we travel in fear, then we hesitate to take the next step into the future. Take it we must, but it is done falteringly, reluctantly, empty of any joyous adventure. Fear makes us look back to better days and ask why they had to evaporate.

The writer dwells upon the word "faith" as the proper stance for the living of these days. Faith, too, looks backwards. But it does so, not with nostalgia, but rather to find the signs of confirmation that life has direction, purpose, and a foundation which is not of this world.

Our writer lists those persons of the Old Covenant — Abel, Enoch, Abraham, to name a few — who looked back upon God's generosity in their lives, or to their nation. Finding assurance of his presence in their past, they marched into the unknown future with the faithful confidence that their God was consistent, not capricious, in his love for his people.

In the last words of the passage we heard together, the writer addresses the Christian:

> *Therefore, looking to Jesus, the pioneer and perfector of our*
> *faith, let us run with perserverance the race that is set before us.*

In faith we look *back to him* who blazed God's trail clearly in the world, and in faith we look *forward with him* who clears away the underbrush of the unknown before us.

Whatever memories we have today of these lives gone awhile from our sight, have meaning for the life beyond our sight because of this Jesus; this Word from God become flesh. He confirms that we are gathered here today as those who stand at the end of the beginning, and that there is prepared for us a city whose builder and maker is God.

HIS OWN KIND OF REPENTANCE
Daniel Shutters

Preached at the funeral of a man whom the writer did not know.

†††

We gather here this morning to pay tribute to Herbert Decker. I didn't know this man personally, and it may seem strange for me to take this few moments to reflect on his life, because of it. However, after talking with some members of his family, I think that there are some things that should be said, some points that are worth remembering.

The first point is that every life is worth something. And it is up to us to try to see it's worth. Herbert fathered a large family. And, to a large degree, his presence and absence influenced how his children grew up. I have gotten the sense that Herbert was an independent man. It takes a good deal of strength to be a loner in this world. And, as I know his children, I would say that they have developed not only their father's strength to be independent, but, also, because of his absence, an awareness of the need to love each other. Stronger, because they had to rely on their own resources, more loving of each other, because they knew what the absence of love meant.

The second point is that each man lives his life as best he knows how, and it is not for us to condemn this man, or any man. Instead, let us try to understand him. I gather from you, his family, that there was bitterness and anger when he left you many years ago. Wrong as that may be, consider his actions after he left you, and what must have been going on inside his mind. He did not desert you entirely, for, while each of you was a child, he contributed financially to your support. He remained in the city. Surely, if he wanted to completely separate himself from you, he could have done so. I suspect that, not only was Herbert a loner, but a very lonely man, filled with guilt feelings most of his life, and not able to ask for forgiveness.

He didn't trust banks or doctors. He was a loner and didn't ask for help. But each of us needs help during our lives, whether it be medical, financial, or the support of friends and family. He denied himself these things. He denied himself the opportunity for forgiveness, the joy of fellowship with his family. he retreated to a small one-room apartment and lived his life cut off from its roots. He was a loner, and couldn't bring himself to ask for help.

He was a bricklayer by trade, but during the last years of his life he worked in a nursery school. A strange combination, but not really, if he missed his children and grandchildren as much as I think he did. I'm told that he worked very hard for the substitute children he found at the school and was very well liked. I prefer to think that here was a man who felt he had wronged his own family and felt that guilt. Here was a man who didn't ask others for help, and found that he didn't know how to ask for forgiveness, even though some of you have said the anger went out of your hearts years ago. Here was a man, who in his last years, tried asking forgiveness by giving someone else's children the love and care he hadn't given his own.

This is Holy Week. At this time we are especially reminded of Christ's death on the cross and the reason for his coming to us. That we might be forgiven of our sins. May I suggest to you that Herbert Decker's mistakes, his self-imposed isolation, and his indirect method of trying to make amends and ask for forgiveness is common to us all, to a greater or lesser degree. By his death, let us all be reminded of our own need for forgiveness and the willingness of Christ to do so.

WHEN A CHRISTIAN DIES
Jerry L. Schmalenberger

Preached at a Sunday morning worship service, one week following the death of a sixty-year-old woman which occurred during the previous Sunday's worship service.

†††

Last Sunday, Mrs. Dwight (Roberta) Keller drove to her church for worship, as was her custom. She had for years helped in the nursery, took part in the church school, and faithfully worshiped as a part of our family of God.

She died while seated in the pew last Sunday during the sermon. The ushers carried her out on a cot. I slipped out while Dr. Frank Seilhamer was preaching and 'had the "commendation of the dying" for her — right behind this altar. We held her funeral Wednesday here, right where she died. Her pall-covered casket sat there in the aisle with the paschal candle light shining upon it. Because that death was a shock, a hurt, and yet such a beautiful thing, we who are a part of her family of God must talk about it today. There were some great lessons acted out right in this place last Sunday and I want to remind you of them.

Our worship here is more than words — there are *grave* implications in all we do around this altar. Roberta Keller's death in our midst was one of God's visual aids. Think of the words she said before she died:

In the confession . . . "increase in us true knowledge of thee and of thy will, and true obedience to thy word, that by thy grace we may come to everlasting life; through Jesus Christ our Lord."

I promised her in the absolution — "He (she) that believeth, and is baptized, shall be saved."

I stepped to the altar and read the Introit from the Psalm: "The sorrows of death compass me . . . in my distress I called upon the Lord: and he heard my voice out of his temple: the Lord is my rock and my fortress."

I prayed in the *collect*, "Oh, Lord, we beseech thee favorably to hear the prayers of thy people that we, who are justly punished for our offenses, may be mercifully delivered by thy goodness . . . "

In *the creed*, she joined me in stating our belief about death: "I believe in the Holy Ghost; the Holy Christian Church, the communion of Saints; the forgiveness of sins; the resurrection of the body, and the life everlasting."

In the *Peace* — another member got up and went over to her and extended her hand in friendship "the peace of the Lord be with you" — "and with you also!" — the last words she said.

Then came the sermon hymn. I had selected it because it talked about the ministry. But verse two said, "as laborers in thy vineyard, Lord, send them out to be content to bear thy burden of weary days for thee; to ask no other wages when thou shalt call them home, but to have shared the travail which make thy kingdom come."

And then she died — the last sound from her throat a hymn to her God. Certainly, in this context, this perspective, we see the preciousness of the things we do called worship. When we come together to worship and study, it's more than another service club — more than enjoying each other's fellowship. Certainly more than a good or bad anthem or sermon. We begin our relationship with God at this font. We deal with things eternal and not only life here but also beyond the grave. How can some say it is old fashioned? How can some cry "irrelevant"? How can any parent claim to let their children decide for themselves?

Certainly more important than home, nation, job, marriage partner, or income; not just a temporary fad or just a good feeling, we are far more than a nice organization that does kind things. We do more than have a moment of silence for the deceased. We handle here the equipment and tools of salvation.

On April 5, 1913, the Rev. Simon Peter Long baptized an infant at this very baptismal font by the name of Roberta Pittinger. Pastor Long pronounced this blessing: "Almighty God, the father of our Lord Jesus Christ, who hath begotten thee again of water and the Holy Ghost, and hath forgiven thee all thy sins, strengthen thee with his grace unto life everlasting." That prayer with that gift was answered last Sunday morning for Roberta Keller. That brings me to the second lesson:

We have a gift to give. What a beautiful thing it   as that Mrs. William Lantz got up and went over to extend "The Peace" to Mrs. Keller who was by herself. We never know what it may mean when we do an act of kindness like that. Let's promise ourselves right now we'll not wait til someone dies to do the nice things. Let's promise we'll put it off no longer, that we'll take the first step, that we'll make the first move, that we'll extend our hand, too, and give God's peace to all of the lonely, or stubborn, or comfortable, within our reach. It won't be necessary to send flowers when they die, because they'll know how we trested them when they lived.

The Contac commercial on TV says:
"Give your hand to a friend and
give your heart to your love,
but give your cold to Contac."
We Christians might put it:
"Give your hand to a friend,
give your heart to your love
and give your life to Jesus Christ."
There are always in our worship service some who will never be back. They die, we die, everyone dies. There are those who try this worship once and decide on that basis whether they'll ever return again. There are always opportunities for us to extend our hand in kind friendship. We always have the opportunity to encourage, to bless, to strengthen and give hope. The peace that comes to the saved and the peace which passes all understanding and the peace of being "in Christ" and the peace we sing about at Christmas and sense after Easter — we pray for and give thanks for — it is ours and we extend it! That's quite a gift we have to give! Indeed, we have a gift to give.

TODAY IS THE DAY OF REPENTANCE: DON'T PROCRASTINATE!
Phillip B. Giessler

Preached upon the death of an elderly woman who, seemingly, was recovering nicely from a broken hip, when she was stricken by a heart attack.

†††

And so, as the Holy Spirit says, Today, if you hear Him speak, don't close your minds as it happened when the people provoked Me at the time they tested me in the desert, where your fathers put Me to a test when for forty years they saw what I could do. That was why I was angry with those people, and I said, "In their hearts they always wander around and never have learned My paths." So because I was angry I swore they will never come to My place of rest! See to it, fellow Christians, that none of you has a wicked, unbelieving heart that turns away from the living God. Yes, *encourage* one another every day, as long as you can say today, to keep sin from deceiving anyone of you with its pleasure and closing your mind to the truth. We share in Christ if we only keep our first confidence unshaken to the end. (Hebrews 3:7-14)

In the Name of Jesus, he who is the Resurrection and the Life, friends of our sister Helena, now fallen asleep, and especially you, the immediate family of a mother, grandmother, and sister now called home.

I.

Who would have guessed just a week ago that we would be here today? But God has arranged it for a purpose. No, that purpose is not to praise our departed Christian sister — though we shall say a few words about her strong faith in Jesus.

Certainly we must speak glory to Christ's Name as the One who has delivered Helena into heavenly mansions above.

But most of all, we gather to have a word spoken to ourselves in preparation of the time we are faced with death.

This means we come to a time of a funeral. Of such a time, J. R. Chiles writes, "Funerals at times can be so faithfully and so prayerfully conducted as to change the destiny of the living. Only that which is true, that which is right, that which is kind, and that which is helpful has any proper place in a funeral service. Faults of the dead are not to be minimized nor false hopes permitted for anybody. Christ is the only Saviour, repentance and faith the only way to get to Him, and the obedience of a spiritual life, the only proper testimony for Him. Ministers are asked to conduct funerals because they preach the word of truth and ought to do so something in line with the calling of God and the expectations of the people."*

Such a Word of Scripture we wish to communicate on the basis of an ancient text meant for our Twentieth Century lives. It deals with death and the danger of *procrastination.*

It says that TODAY is the day for repentance — for, within twenty-four hours, we may be called home as has been Helena.

Are you ready in honest confession of sin and true belief in Jesus?

If you aren't, you are procrastinating! And the only kind of procrastination which the Lord favors is the putting-off-of-sin, not the putting-off-of-belief.

But, since we cannot put off sins of ourselves, but have Christ who has taken them off of us by his death on the cross, we cannot procrastinate concerning *belief.*

That's why the writer of Hebrews says, "And so, as the Holy Spirit says, Today, if you hear him speak, don't close your minds as it happened when the people provoked me at the time they tested Me in the desert, where your fathers put me to a rest when for forty years they saw what I could do."

You can read that story of Israel's foolishness in the Old Testament book of *Numbers.* God passed the test but many Israelites flunked it into hell because they procrastinated — and their TODAYS became the TOMORROWS of death before they were ready.

They closed their minds to Yahweh's warnings and deliberately sinned.

Of it all, God said, "That is why I was angry with those people, and I said, 'In their hearts they always wander around and never have learned my paths.' So because I was angry I swore they will never come to my place of rest!"

And his warning to us is just as sharp. He says, in the text, "See to it, fellow Christians, that none of you has a wicked, unbelieving heart that turns away from the living God."

To heed that warning and pass the test before us calls for the word of *encouragement* in the next verse of the text from Hebrews. The writer says: "Yes, encourage one another every day, as long as you can say TODAY, to keep sin from deceiving any one of you with its pleasure and closing your mind to the truth."

Are any of you deceived at this moment? What are your sins? Does alcoholism have control of you or greed or gossip or laziness or just plain unbelief? Don't play the game of waiting with these sins TODAY. But, rather give those sins to Jesus in confession and take his offer of forgiveness and a new life TODAY before He comes TOMORROW — maybe even TODAY — in death.

Helena took the warning and encouragement many years ago. She knew the truth of the text's final words: "We share in Christ if we only keep our first confidence unshaken to the end."

---

*John R. Chiles, *A Treasure of Funeral Messages* (Grand Rapids: Baker Book House, 1966), p. 15.

II.

TODAY we are alive. God calls us in his mercy — and often calls longer than we deserve.

But don't tempt him. His patience runs out and death sets in. Yes, contrary to the thinking of many Twentieth Century personalities, God is a God of wrath as well as a God of love.

There is a hell for the procrastinator. The cross of Christ shows this. God would not have demanded the death of his Son if sin did not have to be paid for; he would not have forsaken Jesus if transgression could be passed by lightly. So it is that he who does not believe by the truth of Christ's cross is lost.

But the cross shows forgiveness, life, and heaven for those who repent TODAY. Christ's sacrifice destroyed the consequences of hell and you can have the blessings of that today.

Friends, picture a globe the size of our planet — eight thousand miles across made of solid granite. Suppose that a little bird flies to a certain spot only *once* each year and takes one peck. Year after year he pecks in the same spot. Then after one thousand years, a scratch appears on the surface. When that bird has the whole planet pecked away, then eternity will be over. But we know that it will not even be over then.

Do you wish to procrastinate with the chance of spending eternity in the wrong place, missing out on the glories of the heaven Helena has now inherited?

No wonder the Holy Ghost says, "TODAY (as) you hear (God) speak, don't close your minds . . . "

There will be no second chance. Scripture says, "It is appointed unto men once to die and then the judgment." (Hebrews 9:27) And again: "If a tree fall toward the south or toward the north, in the place where the tree falleth, there shall it be." (Ecclesiastes 11:3)

May you be ready for heaven TODAY. AMEN.

THE WONDER OF IMMORTALITY
W. Norman MacFarlane

A sermon on death, preached at a regular Sunday service.

†††

For approximately fifteen centuries, Christendom has expressed the doctrine of immortality in the familiar words of the creed, "I believe in the resurrection of the body and the life everlasting." For many years, Dr. Effie Jane Wheeler taught English Literature at Wheaton College in Illinois. She was noted for her piety as well as her knowledge of the subjects she taught. In May, 1949, on Memorial Day, Dr. Wheeler wrote the following letter to the president of the college, her colleagues, and former students:

> *I greatly appreciate the moment in the chapel that may be given to reading this, for before you leave for the summer I would like to have you know the truth about me as I learned it for myself last Friday. My doctor has at last given me what has been his real diagnosis of my illness for weeks — an inoperable case of cancer. Now if he had been a Christian he wouldn't have been so shaken, for he would have known as you and I do that life or death is equally welcome when we live in the will and presence of the Lord. If the Lord has chosen me to go to him soon, I go gladly. Please do not give a moment's grief for me. I do not say a cold goodbye, but a warm Auf Wiedersehen till I see you again in that blessed land where I may be allowed to draw aside a curtain when you enter.*

Just two weeks after writing this letter, Dr. Wheeler entered the presence of her Lord and Master who had promised to take the sting out of death.

Death is a universal experience, yet many folks will not think about it until compelled to. They are offended by the thought of hell and embarrassed by the thought of heaven. Death comes to every man, pulling kings from their thrones, snuffing out the flickering candle of old age, plucking out the bloom from the soil of humanity and separating the most intimate companions. But whether this is a triumph or a tragedy, depends on whether you can say with absolute conviction and assurance: "I believe in the resurrection of the body and the life everlasting." Father Joseph O'Callahan, who was chaplain of the ill-fated Franklin which was all but sunk off the coast of Japan in 1945, wrote in his book: "Death is not horrible when it becomes a gateway to heaven. Death is horrible only when it strikes one who is turned away from God."

However, let us admit that even Christians do not relish the thought of dying. We all want to go to heaven, but no one is in any hurry to get there. And this is natural; the Bible plainly tells us that death is an enemy. God has put into our natures the instinct of survival. But the wonder of immortality is this that God grants to mortal men the unexplainable gift of eternal life. This is the sum and substance of the Christian gospel; this is why Jesus died and rose again, that whosoever believeth in him should not perish but have everlasting life. Birth, life, and death are the natural order of things. Physical resurrection and immortality are supernatural gifts when God intervenes in the natural process to rescue from eternal death those who have trusted in him for their salvation. When our blessed Lord rose from the dead and ascended to the Father, he called back over the embattlements of heaven "Because I live ye shall live also." The physical death which we have seen and will experience is the cessation of our earthly functions and so we tend to think of it as passing into oblivion. We fight against this by embalming the final remains and buying expensive concrete vaults to extend the semblance of physical life as long as possible. Then as we take our last look at the deceased, it's always nice to remark about how natural they look. There is so much in our funeral procedure that is a denial of everything we profess to believe that we occasionally need to be reminded of the doctrine of immortality.

There has been a great deal of speculation concerning heaven — many extravagant statements, many wild guesses. Often, our funeral procedure involves a lot of flowery rhetoric and vague poetry to which distracted men resort when unbelief seeks to offer comfort and consolation. This morning I advance no theories, no opinions. I promise you no astronomical exactitudes concerning the furniture of heaven or the temperature of hell, but I only seek to present to you the reality and the beauty of the place where one day all of God's people will be reunited. Perhaps Jesus told us so little about our heavenly home because human language is not adequate to convey the eternal glories of the place he has gone to prepare for us. Paul admitted the limitations of language in this regard when he said, "Eye hath not seen, nor ear heard, nor has entered into the heart of man the things which God hath pared for them that love him." Since we know so little of what it is, let us approach the subject negatively and consider what it is not. The wonder of immortality is that we shall dwell in the house of the Lord forever — a place without separation, without limitation, and without termination.

I. Life Without Separation

Many of the heartaches of this present life are caused by separation, and no one knows this better than service families. We dislike saying goodbye even for a short time. The pain of separation is felt even more keenly by millions of families who have been touched by the cold hand of death. Even though that loved one may have died with the sure and certain hope of the resurrection, still those who are left behind are saddened by the separation. The empty chair at the table, the picture on the mantle, voices no longer heard except by the memory — these are all part of the price we have to pay for living in a world of change and decay.

When Jesus was about to be separated from his disciples, he said: "Let not your heart be troubled . . . I go to prepare a place for you . . . I will come again and receive you unto myself that where I am there ye may be also." All the sympathy and comfort extended by friends in the hour of grief cannot dispel the gloom or heal the wounds caused by separation as do these simple words: "I go to prepare a place for you, I will come again, I will receive you unto myself." Hymnwriter John Fawcett expressed it this way:

> When we asunder part it gives us inward pain
> But we shall still be joined in heart
> And hope to meet again.

The long night of sorrow and bereavement has been brightened by the light that comes from the assurance that we shall meet again. What hope this brings to those whose lives have been watered by tears of sorrow, what strength it affords to those who have been weakened by the heavy labors of life. It is the hope of a future reunion at God's throne that takes the sting out of death and enables us to endure the separations of the present. This is what gilds the clouds of life's inevitable sorrows with a heaven sent joy.

Ten years ago, I assisted at a funeral service at the church where I had been pastor. It was a man who had been a Christian only a year and a half, and yet whose life was consistent with everything he believed. The casket rested on the exact spot where I had once seen him stand to give a public confession of his faith in Christ. I began my part of the service with these words: "He is not here, he is risen; for to be absent from the body is to be present with the Lord." It was the most unusual funeral I have ever seen. There was none of the usual hysteria on the part of the family and there was none of the depression I normally experience after such a funeral. As I drove back home, it occurred to me that this was not a funeral in the usual sense, but a coronation; for even as we conducted the service he had already passed through the gates of splendor and was in the presence of the Christ he had so recently come to know and love.

Do you remember in January, 1956, when the five American missionaries were martyred by the Auca Indians in Ecuador? On the afternoon when the wives of these men received final confirmation of the tragedy, even the reporters were moved at the quiet fortitude with which they received the news. One reporter said: "We expected mass hysteria; we are seeing instead an eloquent testimony to the power and beauty of the faith for which these men gave their lives." Instead of a hopeless end, in Christ we have an endless hope. And even though death is still an enemy, our sorrow is moderated by the sure and certain hope of the resurrection, at which time we will see not only our Savior face to face, but also those whom we have "loved long since and lost awhile."

The famous Scottish singer, Harry Lauder, was stunned by a telegram from the War Department informing him that his son had been killed in combat. Because he knew his boy was a Christian, Harry Lauder said: "I would that I could picture to you the joy that lies in the assurance of seeing my boy again." Now this may seem like a strange thing to say, but I don't believe that our reunion with loved ones is going to be the greatest joy of heaven or even one of the greatest joys. Perhaps we believe so now because we are thinking in terms of the natural and earthly. I believe our greatest joy will be when we see our Savior, no longer through a glass darkly, but face to face. At which time all human relationships and earthly joys will pale into insignificance in a life without separation.

II. Life Without Limitation

Every day of our lives we are made to realize our limitations. We find ourselves torn between the mighty magnetisms of right and wrong, the desire to do good and the tendency to do evil. We are caught between the glittering artificialities of the flesh and the seemingly less attractive promptings of the Spirit, between our immediate desires and our ultimate goals. The Latin poet, Ovid, said: "I see and approve the better things of life; the worse things of life I follow." Even St. Paul admitted: "The good that I would, I do not; and the evil that I would not, that I do; O wretched man that I am, who shall deliver me?" We must all admit that there is operative in us a law which leads us to do evil even when good intentions are present. At least most of us will admit this. I had a classmate in college who claimed he hadn't sinned for seven years. I don't know what he was doing for seven years. Maybe he was in a coma, or maybe he just had an extremely broad and generous definition of sin.

The experience of each of us will confirm the statement of Scripture that the Spirit is willing but the flesh is weak. However, we can look forward to a day when we shall be completely delivered from evil and from the sin which doth so easily beset us. In that day, Satan and his hosts shall be destroyed and we shall no longer face the foe. There will be no problems of segregation or desegration, no problems of nationalism, no tears of the oppressed, no cry of the poor to God. Breaking through the gloom of sin and death, and hovering over the seeming finality of the grace there now abides the certainty of the resurrection morning when we shall no longer see through a glass darkly, but face to face; when that which is perfect is come and that which is in part shall be done away.

Also, we shall be free from memories that torment us. Many people go through life never having recovered from something that happened years ago, or never having forgiven themselves for something even though God has. Be assured that nothing in this life can in any way mar the eternal bliss that God has prepared for them that love him. The harrassing pursuits of life with its perplexing cares and bewildering pleasures will be a faded memory. You may carry a burden all through life, but with perfect confidence the believer in Christ may look foward to a life without these limitations. This is something we can believe because it is God's promise, sealed in the cross of Christ, recorded in his words of truth and proved in the benediction of unnumbered lives. We read in Revelation 21:

"God shall wipe away all tears from their eyes and there shall be no more death, neither sorrow nor crying, neither shall there be any more pain for the former things have passed away."

This is the hope that comes to those who are sons of God through faith in and commitment to Christ. This hope provides optimism of heart and buoyancy of spirit. It says that however dark the night, a new day will dawn. It proclaims that Christians have a divine destiny. Death and the grave are not life's weary end. It's this future hope that sustains God's people even though they may have lost the most precious thing in life, and enables them to bear their burdens knowing that eternity will transcend the limitatons of time, and the sufferings of this present time are not worthy to be compared with the glory that shall be revealed in us.

III. Life Without Termination

In 1 Thessalonians 4, Paul gives such a vivid description of the return of Christ that you can almost see the heavens rolled back as a scroll and the Lord descending with a shout, with the voice of the archangel and the trumpet of God. Then he says the dead shall be raised incorruptible and we who are living at that time shall be caught up with them and so shall we ever be with the Lord. When a person believes this clear to the hilt and with all his heart because God says it is so, there comes to him a power that no temptation can imperil and no experience can impeach.

One of the very first records of Christianity outside the New Testament is a letter dated A.D. 112, sent by Pliny the younger who was acting Roman governor in Asia, to Trajan the emperor. The governor reports that in Syria a sect has arisen called the Christians. He says, "These foolish people think they are immortal; they go to their death as to triumph, and no threat of punishment has any effect on them." The assurance of eternal life has been a determining factor in much of the church's history because of people who feared not them who are able to kill the body but are not able to kill the soul. Paul wrote to the church at Corinth: "We shall be changed in a moment, in the twinkling of an eye, for this mortal must put on immortality." Then, that which dies is renewed by something over which death has no power and time has no influence. In a day when armies are on the march again, when governments are topping and values changing, when we are afraid to read tomorrow's headlines, we can thank God that we belong to a kingdom that has no end. John Newton wrote in his hymn, *Amazing Grace:*

> "When we've been there ten thousand years
> Bright, shining as the sun
> We've no less days to sing God's praise
> Than when we first begun."

This is way beyond the grasp of the imagination because we simply can't conceive of anything that has no end. You may wonder how this frail body will persevere throughout eternity since most of us are in pretty bad shape by the time we're thirty. In connection with this, rocket scientist Werhner von Braun said:

> *Science has found that nothing can disappear without a trace. Nature does not know extinction; all it knows is transformation. If God applies this principle to the most minute and insignificant part of his universe, doesn't it make sense to assume that he applies it also to the masterpiece of his creation — the human soul? I think it does. Everything science has taught me and continues to teach me, strengthens my belief in the continuity of our spiritual existence after death.*

With this in mind it doesn't make much difference whether the oatmeal was cold at breakfast or the Red Sox beat the Orioles, or whether you are a VIP or a peasant. What is your life? At the longest, it's just a flicker in the ages.

All this explains the inherent worth of one human soul. We may marvel at the wonder of creation and the seven manmade wonders of the world, but what shall it profit a man if he shall gain the whole world and lose his own soul? "The world passeth away and the lust thereof, but he that doeth the will of God abideth forever." This is why the church proclaims that this life is not all; it's not even very much. There is a life beyond the grave; there is a resurrection, there is immortality; meanwhile life does not consist of the things man possesses, because the created world is but a parenthesis of eternity. This life is only a prelude to eternity and in the light of eternity we are all short timers. Let us, therefore, seek first the kingdom of God and his righteousness.

I hope that this sermon will not only increase our appreciation of things eternal, but will so revise our standards of values that God's will may be done in our lives as it is in heaven. Surpassing all human philosophies and ideologies is the imperishable reality that our Lord has gone to prepare a place for us and will one day come again and receive us unto himself. This is the wonder of immortality.

Looking to that day when we shall be forever with thee, O Lord, help us even now to realize that time is nothing and eternity is everything; that the cares and pleasures of the world are so fleeting, but that the spirit of man is immortal; that the things of the flesh can bring us no lasting satisfaction, and that our only peace is to be at peace with thee. Teach us the futility of things temporal and the enduring value of things eternal.

A GRAVESIDE MEDITATION
Ralph Fotia

A funeral sermon preached to a "normal Sunday morning congregation."

†††

It is always a sad responsibility for me to conduct the graveside service. I am always touched by the sadness, the terrible pain, and the emptiness of those present. The final words are spoken and then we all depart, family and friends filled with deep sorrow.

Each person leaves the cemetery with the emptiness of their private sorrow. Death is especially sad when it comes to one who has shared the same experiences and the same truth. For now there is one less person in this life with whom you can share your truth. The graveside brings us to the painful reality of our loss and the void that cannot be replaced or filled. I often wonder what prior preparation anyone has for such terrible and uprooting times.

This morning I want to engage your thoughts and feelings on a subject that is not popular, but is essential. We need to have some preparation for those difficult days that surely come to each one of us. For we are all traveling this most crowded highway. We all travel the road to death.

One day, many years ago, a group of tribesmen was gathered in the court of King Edward of Northumbria. They had something mysterious to discuss. A group of Christian missionaries had just arrived. The question was, "Shall we give them a hearing?" What would this strange religion offer them? At length a warrior stood up and asked: Can this new religion tell us what happens after death? The life of man is like a swallow flying through this lighted hall. It enters in at one door from the darkness outside and, flitting through the light and warmth, passes through the farther door into the dark unknown beyond. Can your religion solve for us the mystery? What comes to persons in the dark, dim unknown? The old chieftan wanted to know what comes to persons in the dark, dim unknown beyond the grave. He wanted to know exactly and completely and so do we.

Whenever we stand at an open grave and are made aware of our final "resting place," we are not far removed from those who have completed their journey. We are suddenly aware that, in spite of our health and status in life, the clock is running out and our personality will soon be erased from the universe. Because of this awful threat of non-being, we live with anxiety. Much of our energy and time are devoted to reducing that threat of non-being. Even the cosmetics of modern funeral practices attempt to transform the dead into a mask of the living. Each individual attempts to cope with the basic anxiety in his or her own way. Yet none of our attempts to reduce anxiety can adequately deal with our ultimate rendezvous with the grave. "All men are mortal." This classical statement is more than an exercise in reasoning. The fact that I must die makes death a most personal and immediate possibility.

What is the good word?

Most of us have rejected the notion that life on this earth is to be endured because of the rewards and glories of the life to come. We do not find much meaning and comfort for daily life with the notion of "pie in the sky by and by." Christian faith does not offer an easy doctrine of death. Christian faith makes no pretense that dying is not real. Pascal, a devout believer said, "The last act is tragic, however happily all the rest of the play; at the last a little earth is thrown upon our head, and that is the end forever." It is true that one day a group of persons will carry a coffin to a grave and that the one not returning will be you. Yet, the fearful subject of death has no crucial significance in the calendar of the believer in Jesus Christ. The New Testament does not give death any ultimate significance.

The New Testament makes it clear that our destiny is to be with Christ in the heavenly places. Not because we die, but because we are baptized in the victory of Christ that followed Good Friday. Romans 6:3-4: "Have you forgotten that all of us who were baptized into Jesus Christ were, by that very action sharing in his death? We were dead and buried with him in Baptism, so that just as he was raised from the dead by that splendid revelation of the Father's power, so we, too, might rise to a new plane together."

It is neither good religion nor healthy religion to insist that our life on this planet is merely a preparation for the life to come. Nor does life have flavor by living as though the grave is the ultimate destiny. Concentrating on our death takes our eye away from the gift of life. Martin Luther held to a healthy attitude regarding this life and the life to come. "Even if I knew that tomorrow the would would go to pieces, I would still plant my apple tree." John Wesley was once asked what he would do if he knew he was to die on a given date. "I would wake up, eat breakfast, go to such and such a place and preach. In the afternoon, after lunch, I would keep my preaching appointment even as in the morning. Then after a little refreshment, I would go home, go to bed, go to asleep, and awake in glory."

There need be no anxiety of non-being for the risen-in-Christ person. Our physical death is certain, but our spiritual resurrection is also assured. Our death is already behind us. "Christ is Risen." New life in Christ has already begun here and now. To be risen with Christ assures us that death does not have the final word. The grave does not have the victory. We live on tip toe because we belong to Christ and, because we are his, the great enemy — death — cannot defeat us.

Surely we mourn over our dead. Why not? God has given us the gift of compassion and love. Jesus, himself, wept over the grave of his dear friend Lazarus. But we weep and mourn not as those who have no hope. Our weeping is real, our pain is deep, but our faith carries us through the dark days. The assurance of our Heavenly Father's presence brings healing to our hurt. God can and will do the work of healing because he is our Father and his love for us is eternal.

HEAVENLY REAL ESTATE
Paul R. Balliett

The texts and stories used by this pastor for the funeral of a lady real estate salesperson, along with the original poem written by Mr. Balliett, speak from that lady to her family. Mr. Balliett has written more than nine hundred such personal poems across the years.

†††

I'm resting in the sunshine now
The way I know I should,
In a garden filled with beauty
Where the air is always good.
I've obtained a place where real estate
Is priceless and so fine . . .
That friends are always glad to call
And say, "It's just Divine."
While the years on earth pass swiftly
Here we have no fear of Time
For the fears of life have vanished
And the atmosphere's sublime.
Tell my friends I'll always love them
And our God is over all.
So, we'll meet again in Heaven
When they hear the Father's call.
For the flowers and the friendship
And the joys of life we've shared,
There's the sweetest kind of memory
In the faith we've all declared.
So, God bless you all, in passing,
May your days ahead be filled,
With the finest and the truest,
'Til we go where God has willed. PRB (3-29-58)

We gather in the Name of our Lord Jesus Christ to obtain the comforts of God's Promises for his Kingdom that is to come. God, like a loving father, does not intend that any of his children go without good counsel and assurances for life on earth or in Heaven. *Prayer and Lord's Prayer*

So, we share these Scriptures which are God's Word for this time and many occasions in life. Among the most familiar words on the face of the earth are what we know as the Twenty-Third Psalm . . . David's gift of faith to all of the world. "Yes, though I walk through the valley of death I will fear no evil." The valley of the shadow of death . . . for we walk in the shadow of many things throughout all life . . . but learn not to be afraid of shadows . . . and at times even rest in relief in the shadows from the heat of the day.

David lay in the open fields and knew that he had a real responsibility in the caring for the sheep. And while he ate . . . and the sheep grazed . . . he knew there were some dangers of life and death. "Thou preparest a table for me in the presence of mine enemies." At different times the flock had been attacked by a wolf . . . and he beat it off with his rod. Attacked by a lion . . . and he broke its jaws with his rod. Attacked by a bear . . . and he thrust his staff down its throat. He knew that he was alone but not alone for God was with him. "Thy rod and thy staff they do give me comfort." Sufficient tools for the task at hand when given the faith and courage necessary. God does intend that we have the faith and the courage to meet life's times of hardship and loneliness. "Surely goodness and mercy shall follow me all the days of my life . . . and I shall dwell in the house of the Lord forever.

Let us repeat this wonderful Psalm together and sense God's assurances for all who love and believe in him.

It was the custom of one country church to hold its Sunday evening Board meetings after the service, and on those occasions the children were to go home and not wait for the Pastor who was their father. One young lad was spotted by his father after the meeting was under way. "Johnny," said the Pastor, "you go on home, this meeting is going to last till late." Trembling in fear of the cemetary outside the church . . . the lad was uptight with terror when he saw a dark figure on the path through the woods that lay ahead. Then silhouetted against the light of his home in the distance . . . Johnny recognized that it was his older brother walking on ahead of him. At once he ran and caught up with his older brother and took his hand. He then walked confidently homeward, safe in the companionship of his older brother. We are all brothers in Christ . . . who has gone ahead of us on the path . . . and we are meant to feel the security of his Presence and his promises. We'll make it safely through the valley of the shadow . . . for Our Savior saves us. "Let not your heart be troubled . . . neither let it be afraid."

The 121st Psalm me says something of the creditable role of baby-sitters. We are all either blessed by a number who have cared for us in your youngest or oldest years . . . or we have also played that role in caring for others on occasion. The parents leave the children with confidence that they are in good hands . . . and that a pleasant night . . . or week can be spent knowing that the little ones will be rightly cared for in their time away. Often the children look eagerly to the coming of grandma or aunty or whoever is playing the role of their babysitter. It will be a happy time for them, too.

"I will lift up mine eyes to the hills . . . from whence cometh my help. He that keepeth thee will not slumber. He will neither slumber nor sleep. He will protect you from all evil. He will protect your coming and your going from now on."

So may we also surrender our loved ones into God's care who will protect the coming and the going forevermore.

A life story of the things enjoyed and included is ever a part of each service that is meaningful . . . and a poem written for what the individual would say to his dear ones.

*Articles and
Funeral Service
Suggestions*

THE ORDER OF A CHRISTIAN FUNERAL
Phillip B. Giessler

The Invocation

The Prayer
O Lord, almighty God and Father, who of old didst declare: Even to your old age I am he; and even to gray hairs will I carry you; I have made, and I will bear; even I will carry and will deliver you, we thank you that, according to your promise, you have for so many years shown your Christian people innumerable proofs of your faithfulness and mercy. We thank you that you have granted all of them ample time for reflection upon your merciful kindness so that they might drink of that well of water which springeth up into everlasting life. Grant to us all, we beseech you, that we may make ready for the unknown hour and for a blessed departure from this world. Enable us to employ well our allotted time and to work while it is day, ere the night come when no man can work. And at the last do, in love, deliver our souls from despair, and let us fall asleep in peace and obtain the crown of everlasting glory; through Jesus Christ, your Son, our Lord. Amen.

The First Scripture Reading: 1 Corinthians 15:35-44
But somebody will ask, "How do the dead rise? And what kind of body will they have when they come back?"
Just think a little! The seed you sow has to die before it is made alive. And the seed you sow is not the body that it will be, but a bare kernel, maybe wheat or something else. But God gives it the body he wanted it to have, and to each kind of seed its own body. Not all flesh is the same. Human beings have one kind of flesh, animals have another, birds have another, and fish have another kind of flesh. And so there are heavenly bodies and earthly bodies. The shining of the sun is different from the shining of the moon, and the shining of the stars is different again. Even one star shines brighter than another.
That is how it will be when the dead rise. When the body is sown, it decays; when it rises, it can't decay. When it is sown, it isn't wonderful; when it rises, it is wonderful. It is sown weak; it rises strong. It is sown a natural body; it rises a body of the Spirit. Just as there is a natural body, so there is a body of the Spirit.

The First Hymn Reading
I know that my Redeemer lives;
    What comfort this sweet sentence gives!
He lives, he lives, who once was dead;
    He lives, my ever living Head.

He lives to silence all my fears,
    He lives to wipe away my tears,

He lives to calm my troubled heart,
    He lives all blessings to impart.

He lives and grants me daily breath;
    He lives, and I shall conquer death;
He lives my mansion to prepare;
    He lives to bring me safely there.

He lives, all glory to his name!
    He lives, my Jesus, still the same.
Oh, the sweet joy this sentence gives,
    "I know that my Redeemer lives!"

The Second Scripture Reading: 1 Corinthians 15:50-58

I tell you, fellow Christians, flesh and blood can't have a share in God's kingdom, or decay have what doesn't decay.

Now I'll tell you a secret. We're not all going to die, but we're all going to be changed — in a moment, in the twinkling of an eye when the last trumpet sounds. It will sound, and the dead will rise immortal, and we'll be changed. This decaying body will be made one that can't decay, and this dying body must be made one that can't die. When this decaying body is made one that can't decay and this dying body is made one that can't die, then will happen what is written: Death is destroyed in victory!

Where, Death is your victory?

Where, Death, is your sting?

Sin gives death its sting, and the Law gives sin its power. But thank God! He gives us the victory through our Lord Jesus Christ.

Stand firm, then, my dear fellow Christians, and let nothing move you. Always keep on doing a great work for the Lord since you know in the Lord your hard work isn't wasted.

The Second Hymn Reading

Abide with me! Fast falls the eventide;
    The darkness deepens; Lord, with me abide.
When other helpers fail and comforts flee,
    Help of the helpless, Oh, abide with me!

Swift to its close ebbs out life's little day;
    Earth's joy grow dim, its glories pass away;
Change and decay in all around I see.
    O Thou, who changest not, abide with me.

I need Thy presence every passing hour;
    What but Thy grace can foil the Tempter's power?
Who like Thyself my guide and stay can be?
    Through cloud and sunshine, oh, abide with me!

I fear no foe, with Thee at hand to bless;
    Ills have no weight and tears no bitterness.

Where is death's sting? Where, grave, the victory
    I triumph still if Thou abide with me.

Hold Thou Thy cross before my closing eyes,
    Shine through the gloom, and point me to the skies.
Heaven's morning breaks, and earth's vain shadows flee;
    In life, in death, O Lord, abide with me!

The Sermon

The Canticle:
    O, how glorious is that kingdom wherein all the saints do rejoice
with Christ. They are clothed with white robes, and follow the Lamb
whithersoever he goeth.

Lord, now lettest thou thy servant depart in peace:
    according to thy word.
For mine eyes have seen thy salvation:
    which thou hast prepared before the face of all people;
A light to lighten the Gentiles:
    and the glory of thy people Israel.
Glory be to the Father, and to the Son, and to the Holy Ghost:
As it was in the beginning, is now,
    and ever shall be, world without end. Amen.

The Lord's Prayer

The Benediction

DEATH AND THE FUNERAL
Richard K. Avery and Donald S. Marsh

These suggestions are excerpted from IN THE WORSHIP WORKSHOP WITH AVERY AND MARSH, published monthly by the C.S.S. Publishing Company. "Death and the Funeral" is from the July, 1975, issue: Volume III, Issue 7.

†††

Yes, indeed, as much as anything else leaders of worship do, our approach to the crisis of death and the funeral service *needs constant evaluation and re-thinking.* Yes, even if people do say, "It was lovely" after the funeral and "It was so *nice.*" And even if they tell us before the service, "We want it simple, that's what he would have wanted." (Simplicity does allow for imaginative and creative possibilities.) And even if we are committed to certain liturgical traditions, we must evaluate our use of those traditions, and our selection of *which* elements of the tradition.

It is with a very real joy and honor that we have Horace Allen, our good friend, as the first guest contributor to this monthly letter. We have shared many things with Horace, many workshops, many services of worship, many good times. He recently told us about the funeral service that he writes about below. It was so moving to us in so many ways that we had to include it in our issue on "Death and the Funeral." So we asked Horace if he could fit it into his busy schedule to write about his experience. He had it to us in about three days. As he told us, this was something he really wanted to write. Read it once straight through for content and the experience. Then read it again for the ideas with which it is loaded. . . . Enjoy it. Then when you get the chance, meet Horace in the flesh. You will love him, as we do.

WHEN LIFE AND DEATH CONTENDED
by Horace T. Allen, Jr.
Associate for Worship
The Program Agency, United Presbyterian Church

This is a very personal witness to the power of Christian worship. It is an account of a funeral of an eighteen-year-old lad, the eldest son of my closest friends. His name was Philip. He was tragically killed a few months ago in an accident involving a tractor on his parents' farm in West Virginia. Philip was a happy, handsome friend of many. His longish blond hair was as bright as his sense of humor. With his parents I had watched him grow from the crib to college. He is survived by two younger brothers and a sister as well as his parents. Because his parents and I went into the ministry together, all those children grew up knowing "Horace." Indeed, it was my "fatherly" joy to have baptized all three of those later children.

So, the news of his sudden death, given me by a close and mutual friend late the night of January 11th, was the kind of body blow that draws tears even before you begin to feel all the grief and contradiction. It is the kind of news that you know instinctively is going, in some significant way, to change your life.

The funeral was set for the morning of January 14th — my forty-second birth — at an Episcopal church in Washington, D.C., St. Stephen's and the Incarnation, where we had all worshiped together so many times. The rector, Father William Wendt, made only one major suggestion about the service: that it be a eucharist, a celebration of Holy Communion. For the rest he turned to the two brothers, Tim and Charles, the sister, Pasty, and a very talented young woman on the parish Liturgy Commission, a friend of the entire family. They were to put that eucharistic liturgy together in terms of hymn selection, officients, readings, etc. That's the way the worship is fashioned there — freedom for creativity within a certain historic structure.

So, Father Wendt was to be celebrant. Professor Paul Lehmann, theological "guru" to many of us, a kind of "father in God," would read the gospel lesson and give the final blessing. A black minister friend of all would preside at the beginning — that day in fact, he had us all stand in silence after the procession to remember a good, glad moment with young Philip. Many other clerical comrades would assist at giving bread and the cup. I was asked to preach. Patsy, dressed in a wonderful long dress, would carry the cross. Charles would read the Epistle (1 Corinthians 13:5-13); Timmy, a family "paper." A number of Philip's prep school and college friends carried the plain pine box covered only with a white cloth embroidered with a big cross.

That box had rested at home in a sun porch during the intervening days as so many people came and went. We all got a little used to it, with its few plants and one lighted candle.

Then came the day for worship, the 14th. We did what people always do at such time: we came close together. We filled the church: Jews, Protestants and Catholics, black and white, many young and some very old, colleagues, friends, cronies, and classmates.

We came together . . . around our "holy things": the Bible, the table, candles, hymns, and that box with its precious burden. Patsy led the procession right down the center aisle, holding the cross high. Philip's friends struggled with the weight of the coffin. Then the family and we ministers, we "servants" of the Word of God.

Channing Phillips had us stand quietly in remembrance at the beginning. We "made a memorial" of our friend. Then sentences from scripture and a prayer. All sat and Tim came to the lectern to read a brief appreciation of their brother: how he had always been "the first to try something" and liked little children, and let you be yourself. The "memorial" was complete.

Ernest Gibson, a Baptist pastor, read from the Old Testament. Charles then read the Epistle, his voice caught only once at "but now I am a man." We sang "A Mighty Fortress" as the gospel procession took the Bible, candles, and incense out into the center aisle, there in front of the coffin with its candles. Dr. Lehmann proclaimed the Gospel, John 20, which included my text: the risen Christ saying, "Peace be with you." *Shalom.*

Now, I had to preach on that text. How? I had it all written out, don't trust either personal and pious improvisations in such a moment. But could I go through with it? There were Philip and Marsha, without their eldest, with each other and the other three. There were so many dear friends and a good many strangers also. There was my theological teacher and the friend who had first given me this news and had sat up with me all that night. Could I?

Shalom, Horace. Look at Charles and Tim and Patsy. The minute you finished the short prayer in the pulpit, they all moved forward on their pews, elbows on knees and chins cupped in hands. You've seen them sit like that before. They're expecting something from you and that Word you serve. And their parents have now relaxed just a little.

So Jesus' words were spoken again, into another room where we had gathered because of a death. "Peace be with you." After drawing what lines I could from our room to that room, from us to the first church, I came to Christ's baptism into death, and ours. And then I told the congregation of my favorite recollection or "memorial" of Philip: how it had troubled him a little that, though I had baptized the other three children, he had been baptized a few months before I had gotten to know his parents. How, at the Easter Vigil Service there at St. Stephen's just two years ago, when I was assisting Father Wendt in signing the worshipers on their foreheads with water to remind them of their baptism, there, first in line was Philip. I splashed water on his forehead and said, "Philip, remember your baptism." He said, "Now you've done me, too."

At the end of the sermon we all sang the Hebrew song, "Shalom," quietly. But it was nice *doing* something together. The text: "Shalom, my friend, shalom. We'll see you again. Shalom."

That word was the door to the table. Father Wendt invited all to greet one another, and to come forward about the table. In doing so we met the family and saw the box. Singing, chanting, thanksgiving . . . then the giving and sharing of bread and wine, signs of life and joy, instruments and sacraments of community and love. All the while, words of peace and comfort and appreciation were being shared with the parents, and with one another — until the blessing. Then Paul Lehmann went right to the coffin in front of the table. He leaned lightly on it and spoke directly to the family, addressing each by name, a personal word of encouragement and then the blessing.

Recessional: cross, clergy, pallbearers, everyone singing "The Strife Is O'er, the Battle Done."

A cemetery — cold. Father Wendt read the kind words of commital and finally invited anyone who wished, to shovel on some dirt . . . that is, physically to "tuck in" our friend. And I noticed how anyone who did, did it in their own individual and very personal way.

Then home, to the uncertain but certainly different future. All manner of things have happened to many of us, even in the few months since then. But some grateful and devout reflections remain.

Christian worship has healing power. That power, however, depends on a number of important continuing tasks:
— learning to sing and to pray together,
— making children and the young "at home" in worship,
— fashioning worship together, regularly,
— keeping the Scriptures alive among us,
— trusting the pastoral office,
— holding together liturgy and life, nurture and worship, personality and prayer,
— facing reality head on,
— taking the sacraments seriously as bearers of identity and identification.

A picture of Philip now graces and gladdens my desk. Is it an icon? If Christ be risen, so is he. And the great Lutheran Easter choral is believable: "It was a strange and dreadful strife, when life and death contended; the victory remained with life, the reign of death was ended."

FUNERALS SHOULD BE CONDUCTED IN THE CHURCH
Lovett Hayes Weems, Jr.

There was a time when almost all funerals were conducted in a church. However, in recent years, the trend has been for more and more funerals to be held from a funeral home "chapel." In some cities the church funeral has almost disappeared completely.

It is generally accepted that the nonchurch funeral is less time consuming and more convenient, especially for the funeral directors. But are these the only factors to be considered by a Christian in determining where his funeral or the funeral of a member of his family should be held?

I believe there are several reasons why a Christian should choose to have his funeral from a church.

First, the church is the place at which the key events in a Christian's life are celebrated. Baptism occurs in the church building, as does confirmation and reception into church membership. Christian weddings usually take place in the church. Therefore, it is altogether proper that one's funeral worship service also be conducted from the church.

Second, one's positive Christian witness can continue, even through the funeral, if the funeral is held from his church. A church funeral will bear witness to the important place that the church held in the person's life. The importance of the church in his life will be stamped much more into the minds of family and friends if the funeral is set in the context of the church.

Third, funeral home "chapels" are almost always devoid of the Christian symbols which are at the heart of faith and worship. This is understandable, of course. The funeral home must be planned in such a way as to serve, without offense, people from varying religious perspectives. This lack of symbols, though understandable, adds another key reason for church funerals.

Fourth, many funeral home "chapels" have a special section in which the family sits during the funeral service. Often the family section is located physcially separate from the section in which the friends sit. In fact, this arrangement often serves actually *to hide* the family from the friends. The reason given for such seating is to provide the family with privacy.

While the need for privacy is important, there is another important consideration for the Christian at this point. Christian people believe that we go through all experiences of life not as "family" and "friends" but as fellow members of God's covenant community. In a time of sorrow, Christian people join together to express love and concern. We do not experience sorrow in isolation but in community. As the Bible says, "If one member suffers, all suffer together; if one member is honored, all rejoice together."

Althought even in a church funeral the family usually sits as a group, there is a big difference. In a church the family does not find itself isolated and hidden but rather literally "surrounded" by fellow Christians who are sharing the sorrow.

Fifth, hymnals and worship aids are not available at funeral homes. Their absence severely limits the content of the funeral worship service. For instance, hymn singing and other acts of worship in which the congregation participates are usually ruled out. This is tragic because it contributes to the trend in which the funeral service contains little more than a eulogy or sermonette and the people present are mere spectators.

Sixth, the church and its ministry usually have less control over the funeral worship service when it is held from a funeral home. Though many times this is not a serious problem, difficulties can arise when funeral home practice differs from that of a particular church or minister.

The church funeral just may be one tradition that we need to recover.

MY APPROACH TO FUNERALS
Larry Eisenberg

I do not usually preach a funeral sermon. Rather, I use Scripture, prayers, and a human interest sketch of the person, usually interposing a few lines about death and its meaning to the living, about Christian faith and the call upon us all to be ready by living in close relationship with Jesus Christ.

I use Scripture sentences:

Jesus said, "I am the resurrection and the life . . . " (John 11:25-26)

"The eternal God is your dwelling place, and underneath are the everlasting arms. (Deuteronomy 33:27)

"The Lord is my light and my salvation . . . " (Psalma 27:1)

"For we know that if the earthly tent we live in . . . " (2 Corinthians 5:1)

Then I usually have a prayer, followed by music. For the second reading, I select among these:

Psalms 27: "The Lord is my Light and my Salvation . . . "

Psalms 121: "I lift up my eyes to the hills . . . "

John 14:1-7: "Let not your heart be troubled"

Romans 8:14-18; 28; 37-39: "All who are led by the Spirit of God . . . All things work together for good . . . Nothing shall separate us . . ."

Next, I may have some more music.

Next is the obituary, and then from notes I have taken from the family about the deceased (in case they are not known to me) I try to include some "human interest" material. What did they like? What were favorite occupations? How were they helpful to humanity? What kind of church member? Even humorous things. What poetry did they like? If available, I get the poetry and read it.

Almost invariably, I end by having all present say Psalm Twenty-Three, introducing it as the greatest affirmation ever written.

On occasion I have given time for people present to respond to their memory of the deceased. "What do you recall about the person that made them great in your eyes, or dear to your memory?" Even when people are overcome with grief, some can respond, and it is meaningful.

At the funeral of my brother-in-law, a seventy-nine-old retired Army colonel in the town where he had lived for twenty-five years, I had the relatives stand, one at a time, and tell the people what their names were and their relationships to the deceased. Later, I asked all to respond to his memory, standing not behind the pulpit but on the level with the people in a small church seating a little over one hundred. They responded for several minutes, and it was meaningful both to the community people and the family.

Also, I have found effective, after the brief graveside service, to lead the people without accompaniment in the chorus of "How Great Thou Art." It gives them a chance to participate, and to reiterate their faith.

THE CONTRIBUTORS

The contributors are listed in the order in which their contributions appear in this volume.

Charles L. Koester is pastor of Holy Trinity Church, West Allis, Wisconsin.

Edward R. Mangelsdorf is pastor of Concordia Lutheran Church, Kendall, New York.

James D. Schmidt is pastor of St. John Lutheran Church, Warren, Ohio.

Kieth Gerberding is pastor of Peace Lutheran Church, Southgate, Michigan.

Lawrence Ruegg is pastor of Faith Lutheran Church, Walworth, Wisconsin.

Carroll R. Gunkel is pastor of University United Methodist Church, College Park, Maryland.

Robert S. Kinsey is pastor of Trinity Lutheran Church, Ashland, Ohio.

Phillip B. Giessler is pastor of St. Thomas Lutheran Church, Rocky River, Ohio.

George L. Bell is pastor of First United Presbyterian Church, Huron, Ohio.

Frank L. Starkey is pastor of House of Prayer Lutheran Church, Escondido, California.

Carl B. Rife is pastor of Brook Hill United Methodist Church, Frederick, Maryland.

Michael L. Sherer is pastor of Redeemer Lutheran Church, Washburn, Iowa.

David A. MacLennan is pastor emeritus of First United Presbyterian Church, Pompano Beach, Florida.

R. Blaine Detrick is pastor of First United Methodist Church, Parkersburg, West Virginia.

Leif Monson is pastor of Walnut Grove, Minnesota.

O. Garfield Beckstrand II is pastor of Trinity Lutheran Church, Rockford, Illinois.

John R. Brokhoff is pastor of homiletics, Candler School of Theology, Emory University, Atlanta, Georgia.

Don R. Yocom is pastor of Epworth United Methodist Church, Lima, Ohio.

Heth H. Corl is pastor of John Stewart United Methodist Church, Upper Sandusky, Ohio.

T. A. Kantonen is professor of systematic theology, retired, Hamma School of Theology, Springfield, Ohio.

Roger L. Tappert is pastor of St. John Lutheran Church, Sunman, Indiana.

James A. Ray is pastor of Faith Lutheran Church, Toledo, Ohio.

Arley Fadness is pastor of Salem Lutheran Church, Parkston, South Dakota.

Edwin R. Lincoln is senior pastor of First Congregational Church, Guilford, Connecticut.

Daniel Shutters is pastor of St. John's Lutheran Church, Steelton. Pennsylvania.

Jerry L. Schmalenberger is pastor of First Lutheran Church, Mansfield, Ohio.

W. Norman MacFarlane is pastor of Phillipus United Church of Christ, Cincinnati, Ohio.

Ralph Fotia is pastor of Shaffer Memorial United Methodist Church, Cleveland, Ohio.

Paul R. Balliett is pastor of Maple Heights United Methodist Church, Maple Heights, Ohio.

Richard K. Avery and Donald S. Marsh are pastor and choir director, respectively, of a Presbyterian congregation in Port Jervis, New York, and are leaders of worship workshops across the country.

Lovett Hayes Weems, Jr., is pastor of the Raleigh United Methodist Church, Raleigh, Mississippi.

Larry Eisenberg is pastor of Grace United Methodist Church, Altus, Oklahoma.